Easy Terms

A comedy

Frank Vickery

Samuel French — London
New York - Toronto - Hollywood

EASY TERMS

First performed by Spectacle Theatre Company at the Dylan Thomas Theatre, Swansea, on 3rd September 1982, with the following cast:

Vi	Lynn Hunter
Howard	Bill Lynn
Mr Fowler	Richard Locke
Adele	Terri O'Donoghue

Directed by Joan Mills
Designed by Kim Kenny
Stage Manager Pippa Boss

Subsequently performed by Grassroots Productions at the Sherman Theatre, Cardiff, on 9th September 1996 with the following cast:

Vi	Helen Griffin
Howard	Daniel Evans
Mr Fowler	Ian Jeffs
Adele	Christine Morris

Directed by Frank Vickery

CHARACTERS

Vi, mid-50s
Howard, Vi's son, early 20s
Mr Fowler (Bernard), early 30s
Adele, young
Girl, non-speaking, young

The action of the play takes place in Vi's and Howard's home and in various settings around a caravan park in Tenby

Time — the present

Other plays by Frank Vickery
published by Samuel French Ltd

Full length:
All's Fair
Biting the Bullet
Breaking the String
Erogenous Zones
Family Planning
A Kiss on the Bottom
Loose Ends
Love Forty
A Night on the Tiles
One O'Clock from the House
Roots and Wings
Spanish Lies
Trivial Pursuits

One act:
After I'm Gone
Green Favours
A Night Out
Split Ends

SYNOPSIS OF SCENES

The play is in two acts made up of seventeen scenes which span the total of about a year

ACT I

SCENE 1 Vi's and Howard's living-room,
   early July
SCENE 2 Vi's and Howard's living-room
SCENE 3 Vi's and Howard's living-room
SCENE 4 Voice-over
SCENE 5 Holiday coach
SCENE 6 Caravan site
SCENE 7 Caravan site
SCENE 8 Telephone box
SCENE 9 Inside the caravan

ACT II

SCENE 1 Open area
SCENE 2 Beach
SCENE 3 Shopping centre/Beach/Outside the
 caravan
SCENE 4 Pub
SCENE 5 Outside the caravan
SCENE 6 Coach
SCENE 7 Outside Vi's and Howard's house
SCENE 8 Vi's new living-room

ACT I

Scene 1

Towards the back of the stage are two very tall and very wide flats which are angled in slightly. Each has a scene painted on it. One depicts a valley setting reflecting the sort of world Vi lives in, the other is a caravan site somewhere in Tenby. These flats remain constant throughout the play

On the floor is a large oblong carpet. Painted on the floor under this, and unseen for the time being, is a huge postcard. It is addressed to Bernard and is signed by Howard and should read, "Dear Bernard, Having a nice time, weather not too bad, looking forward to Thursday, Howard."

The play begins in Vi's and Howard's living-room. Placed on the carpet are two fireside chairs. To the side of each chair is a small table. On the left table (Howard's) is an open packet of sweets and a telephone. On the right table (Vi's) is a cup and saucer with some tea in it. There is a walking stick hooked to the right arm of Vi's chair. There is also the suggestion of a coal fire with fire irons et cetera

Music begins to play. It should be something for violin and cello. The house Lights go down

The stage Lights come up. It is an evening in early July. Howard and Vi are sitting in their respective chairs. Vi is a woman in her mid-fifties but could look slightly older or younger. She has suffered a stroke a year ago and has not regained the full use of her left arm and leg. Howard is a young man in his early twenties

Howard is reading a book and eating an apple. He is preoccupied with his book, although he and his mother are playing a game of "I Spy". Vi's eyes are scanning the room and full of concentration

Vi (*eventually*) Ceiling!
Howard (*without looking up*) No. (*He takes another bite of his apple*)

There is a pause

Vi (*trying to work it out*) It's not carpet, you said.

Howard (*with a mouthful of apple*) No, it's not carpet.

Vi Curtains?

Howard No.

Vi (*after a slight pause*) I know ... kitchen!

Howard (*slowly looking up from his book*) Since when does kitchen start with a "C"? And anyway, tangible things we agreed on.

Vi The kitchen is tangible.

Howard No it's not.

Vi Tangible means you can touch it, right?

Howard Yes.

Vi Well, I can touch the kitchen.

Howard (*laughing*) No, you can't.

Vi Don't tell me ...

Howard All right, what can you touch in there that's specifically the kitchen, then? Go on — answer me that.

Vi (*after a slight pause*) The table.

Howard The table isn't the kitchen. The table's the table.

Vi The cooker.

Howard The same applies.

Vi The walls then. I can touch the bloody walls.

Howard Walls don't make a kitchen.

Vi A kitchen would look hellish funny without them.

Howard Walls make a room.

Vi And a room makes a kitchen.

Howard They also make a bedroom, a bathroom ——

Vi But they don't start with a "C".

Howard Neither does kitchen!

Vi Oh, I give up — it's a bloody silly game anyway.

Howard (*going back to his book*) You asked to play it.

Vi (*after a slight pause*) You didn't have to say yes.

Howard (*without looking up*) I said yes because it's easier than saying no.

Vi (*looking at him; almost goading him*) How is it easier to say yes than no? I can say them both easy enough. Yes, no, yes, no, yes, no, yes ——

Howard Are you playing me up?

Vi (*after a slight pause*) No. (*She laughs*)

Howard joins in with the laugh. There is a slight pause

Howard Shall I put the telly back on?

Vi I've gone off it. It's bad enough in the winter but there's bugger all on through the summer.

Howard (*after a slight pause*) Why don't you have an early night?

Vi Why don't you?

Howard I'm not tired.
Vi Neither am I.

They look at each other. There is a pause between them. A moment passes before Howard returns to his book

(*Holding the stare; after a pause*) I still can't get over you.

Howard slowly looks up at her

Fancy booking that caravan without even asking me.
Howard I'm paying for it.
Vi That's not the point ... How do you know I'll go?
Howard (*returning to his book, knowing what game she's playing*) It won't matter if you don't — I'll go on my own.
Vi You said you hired it for me.
Howard I did, but I've paid for it now and I'm not going to waste it.
Vi But you couldn't leave me to manage on my own.
Howard Why not?
Vi I wouldn't be able to cope.
Howard Not in this house perhaps, not with the stairs.

A slight pause

(*Playing her at her own game*) The Social Services have got places to take people like you in — you know, to give the rest of the family a break, a week or so away.
Vi (*outraged*) You'd put me away just to have a week on your own in a caravan?
Howard If you wouldn't come with me I would, yes.
Vi You never cease to amaze me. I always knew ... Your father always said you'd grow up to be a hard bugger. You haven't got a heart: a swinging brick, that's what you've got.
Howard Look, let's not kid each other. You know I've got no intention of going to the caravan on my own, and I know you've got no intention of letting me.

They stare at each other for a moment. Vi eventually backs off; she smiles but covers it and looks away. Howard returns to his book. After a moment and without looking up, he reaches for a sweet out of the packet. The noise of this makes Vi look in his direction. Howard senses her glare and looks up at her. They stare at each other again. Vi's eyes move frantically from Howard's face to the packet of sweets on the small table. Howard knows she wants one;

he sighs, smiles and throws a sweet towards Vi. The sweet lands on her lap and with the aid of the gammy hand she unwraps it and pops it into her mouth

Vi Do you think a week is long enough?
Howard Would you like to stay longer?
Vi I always think a fortnight is too long.
Howard Leave it at a week then.
Vi Do you fancy a fortnight?
Howard Not really.
Vi They say a fortnight's always best.
Howard Who does?
Vi It takes a week to settle in and find the place.
Howard We'll have a fortnight then.
Vi Won't the caravan be booked?
Howard It's possible — we'll have to take a week in another one.
Vi Oh, I'm not changing horses mid-flight. Leave it at a week and we'll stay as we are. (*Suddenly she shouts*) Candles!
Howard What?
Vi Candles. They begin with a "C".
Howard (*smiling*) I thought you'd given up.
Vi It is that, isn't it?
Howard (*quickly looking around*) I don't see any candles.
Vi They're in one of the sideboard drawers.
Howard It's got to be something in sight. Those are the rules.
Vi Rules. You've always got to do everything by the rules.
Howard It's the only fair way to play.
Vi You've always been the same; honest to a fault. Life's no fun unless you cheat a bit.
Howard (*almost challenging her*) How do you know I haven't cheated?
Vi I'm not talking about "I Spy".
Howard Neither am I.
Vi (*after a slight pause*) Have you? Cheated?

Now is Howard's chance to say something. There is a slight pause

Howard No — not yet. (*He backs off*) You're right though. I do live by the rules — but I might not always. I can cheat as good as you if I want to. (*He puts his book down*)

Howard walks off R into the kitchen

Vi Do you think I cheat you?
Howard (*off*) Yes.

Vi When?
Howard (*off*) All the time.
Vi When?
Howard (*off*) Every day. Right. Cocoa or tea?

There is a slight pause

Vi I spy with my little eye, something's beginning with Howard.

Black-out. Violin music plays, overlapping with, then superceded by, a local radio station

SCENE 2

The living-room

The Lights come up; the radio sound fades to a very quiet background noise coming from an onstage radio. There is an insurance account book on the small table by the chair DL

Vi is pushing a Ewbank sweeper over the carpet

Suddenly there is a knock on the door

Vi (*calling*) Come in ... it's open.

Bernard Fowler, the insurance man, comes into the room. He is not a bad looking man, possibly in his early thirties. He carries an attaché case and is wearing a suit, shirt and tie

Bernard Hallo. How are you, Mrs Davies?
Vi All right. You're early this morning. Didn't stay long in next door, did you?
Bernard Couldn't get an answer.
Vi Funny, 'cause they are there. I heard them about ten minutes ago. There's the book there. (*She points to the insurance book*) The money's on the side.
Bernard Where's Howard?
Vi I've just sent him down Jones's. He had cornflakes this morning and took all the milk.
Bernard (*sitting in the chair* L) No cuppa for me today, then.
Vi Unless you can drink it without.
Bernard Will he be long?
Vi It depends. He's been like Dilly bloody Daydream this last fortnight.

Bernard I think I'll wait. I'm quite parched.

Vi Go and do the rest of the street if you like. Tea should be on the table by the time you come back. (*She indicates Bernard's legs*) Up.

Bernard raises both legs so that Vi can Ewbank under them. During the following he busies himself with the paperwork associated with Vi's insurance

Bernard I've done them all. I go to Maindy Grove next and there's no chance of a cuppa there.

Vi Better wait then. He shouldn't be long, I must have sent him ten minutes ago.

Bernard Yes, I thought I saw him walking down the road as I was going into number thirty-four.

Vi (*placing the Ewbank* UR) Hey, she's had new furniture, hasn't she? Number thirty-four?

Bernard (*covering a smile*) I think so, yes.

Vi Must have come into a bit of money then.

Bernard An endowment matured.

Vi I've got one coming up, haven't I?

Bernard (*filling in the card*) I'll tell you now.

Vi (*going to him*) Oh, while I remember — we won't be here next week.

Bernard Yes, that's right.

Vi How do you know?

Bernard (*after a slight pause*) What?

Vi That we won't be here next week.

Bernard (*after a slight pause*) Well, you're going to Tenby. To the caravan.

Vi Who told you?

Bernard Er ... Howard. Howard said.

Vi I thought you only saw him as you were going into number thirty-four.

Bernard Last week. He mentioned it last week.

Vi Did he now? He didn't say anything to me until three days ago.

Bernard He wanted to surprise you, I expect. (*He pauses slightly, swallowing hard*) April next year.

Vi What's that?

Bernard April next year. You've got an endowment coming out on Howard. Listen, on second thoughts, I won't wait for that tea. Better press on. (*He stands*) Have a nice holiday and I'll — er — I'll see you when you get back.

Vi Howard won't be a minute now.

Bernard No, it's all right — honest.

Howard (*off; calling*) Mam?

Vi There he is.

Howard (*off*) Has the insurance man ... ?

Howard enters with a bottle of milk

(*Seeing Bernard*) Oh ... there you are. We ran out of milk.

Bernard I'll see you both when you get back.

Howard Aren't you going to have any tea?

Bernard No. I'll — er — have to go.

Howard It won't take two minutes.

Bernard Better get on. Hope everything goes all right for you. I'll see you both. (*He turns and heads for the exit*)

Howard But ...

Vi Ta-ra.

Bernard exits

Vi sits in the chair R. Howard stands with his back to Vi, looking after Bernard

I meant to have told you to get bread at the same time, Howard.

Howard (*almost snapping at her*) There's bread here.

Vi Put the kettle on. We'll have a cup of tea anyway, shall we?

Howard (*turning to face Vi*) Yeah, but you can put it on.

Vi (*reluctantly*) Have I got to?

Howard Therapy for you.

Vi I can't get on with that cooker.

Howard Make yourself get on with it. You shouldn't rely on me to do everything. You know what the physiotherapist told you. You've got to do more or you'll never get the use of that hand back. (*He holds out the bottle of milk*)

Vi reluctantly takes it. She makes a real meal of getting out of the chair

Vi You're hard, you are.

Vi exits to the kitchen

Howard has a brief moment alone. He takes off his jacket and places it on the back of the chair L

(*Off*) I've got some money coming out on you next April ... It's not a lot, but what shall we do with it?

Howard doesn't answer

(*Off*) Howard, can you hear me? Are you there, Howard? (*She shouts*)
Howard!

Howard (*shouting back*) What!

Vi (*off*) Are you there?

Howard Of course I'm here — where the hell do you think I am? (*He crosses
and switches off the radio*)

Vi enters

Vi Well, answer me then. (*She stops and looks at Howard*) Told him we had
a caravan last week, then, did you?

Howard (*backing off*) Well, I could hardly get the caravan without him
knowing.

Vi Why not?

Howard He owns it.

Vi (*shocked*) Well, he never said.

Howard Did you ask him?

Vi No, but ——

Howard (*getting the Ewbank and starting to use it*) Well, there you are then.

Vi How much did he charge you?

Howard (*working away* DL) I can't remember.

Vi It's hardly something you'd forget.

Howard A hundred pounds. A hundred pounds for the week.

Vi (*following Howard*) Where did you get a hundred pounds from?

Howard I saved it.

Vi That's a lot of money.

Howard (*working away across the front*, R) Not today it's not.

Vi Have you paid him?

Howard Yes, of course I've paid him.

Vi (*following Howard*) You think he'd have let us have it a bit cheaper,
seeing as he knows us.

Howard He did. He normally charges double.

Vi Funny how he never mentioned he had a caravan before.

Howard Not really. (*He eases away from Vi, moving behind the chair and
crossing back* R)

Vi How did you find out then?

Howard He told me.

Vi When?

Howard A long time ago.

Vi When?

Howard (*snapping*) Last March. The second of bloody March. A Tuesday,
twenty past eleven a.m.. You'd lost one of the payment cards, and while

you were in the front room, ripping the sideboard apart, me and the insurance man made chit-chat over a cup of tea. Milky, two sugars, on the weak side.

There is a slight pause. Vi looks at Howard

Vi The second of March was a Friday.

Howard, frustrated, replaces the Ewbank and exits into the kitchen

You lost the card, not me, and it's weak with one sugar not two. (*A slight pause*) And I just Ewbanked not five minutes before you came in. (*She smiles to herself and sits back down in her chair. A slight pause*) Are you making tea, Howard?
Howard No!
Vi Oh, go on. You make the tea now, and I'll make the cocoa later on.

Howard enters from the kitchen and confronts Vi

Howard I'm putting my foot down. I've been too soft with you. You've got to start doing more.
Vi I don't see the point. Not while you're here to do it for me.
Howard I might not always be here.
Vi Oh, I'll go before you do, don't you worry.
Howard I didn't mean die.
Vi (*after a slight pause*) Where are you going then?
Howard Nowhere. I'm not going anywhere — but you shouldn't rely on me so much.
Vi Well, if a mother can't rely on her own son ...
Howard (*kneeling* UL *of Vi's chair*) I'm not complaining — I just want what's best for you.
Vi (*sighing*) Oh, it's this place, Howard. It doesn't give me no heart. Perhaps I'd try a bit more if I had one of them new housing association flats.

Howard gets up excitedly and sits on the arm of the chair, putting his arm along the back

Howard Hey, did I tell you I went to the offices again this week? They're sending a man round.
Vi I've got no time for them council men.
Howard He's not coming to see you, he's coming to see the house.

Vi What's he want to look at the house for?

Howard He wants to see how badly in need of repair it is.

Vi Do you think they'll do it up? Perhaps we'll have one of them grants: what do you think?

Howard I think they're more likely to pull it down — before it falls down around our feet.

Vi It was a good house once.

Howard Ay, forty years ago.

Vi You don't reckon they'll spend money on it then?

Howard I imagine the building inspector will take one look at this and slap a closing order on it.

Vi Well, I hope he doesn't slap it on the pine end or the whole bloody lot will come down.

They both laugh. There is a slight pause. Howard moves to stand behind Vi's chair. He leans over the back to talk to her

Howard You — er — you fancy one of them housing association flats then, do you?

Vi Oh, I think they're lovely.

Howard Central heating.

Vi Nice clean walls.

Howard Toilet and bathroom.

Vi Doors that shut.

Howard Friendly neighbours.

Vi Friendly neighbours.

Howard You fancy all that then?

Vi Oh yes.

Howard Good.

Vi I think we'd be very happy in one of those, Howard.

Howard looks up and out. His expression is one of despair

Black-out. Violin music plays

Scene 3

The living-room

The Lights come up; the music changes to the "Emmerdale" theme

Howard's shirt is on the back of a dining chair, airing in front of the fire. His shoes are onstage too

Vi is sitting in her armchair. She is wearing a dressing-gown and has a TV remote control unit in her hand

Howard enters from the kitchen with a towel around his neck. He is half dressed

Howard (*drying his hair, looking in an imaginary mirror*) I've left everything out in the kitchen for you so if you fancy a cuppa later on you've only got to light the gas.

Vi Suppose I can't get out of this chair?

Howard Suppose I was to drop dead? Look, I'm only going out for an hour.

Vi You said that last Thursday.

Howard An hour once a week.

Vi Oh, it's going to be a regular thing now, is it?

Howard You shouldn't complain.

Vi I'm not complaining. I just want to know where I stand that's all.

Howard I'm having a night out. I need a break.

Vi (*accusingly*) From who?

Howard The house.

Vi Me, you mean.

Howard Yes, from you. Why not.

Vi (*after a slight pause*) You always used to be a home bird. I can remember a time when me and your father had to drag you out to the toilet. It was only because of you we thought of having one put upstairs. And look at you now — can't keep you in. (*A pause*) I hope you've left the matches where I can find them.

Howard You don't need them with that cooker, I've told you before. Just turn the knob and press the little red button.

Vi Now you know I can't mess with them things. You put the matches out — I'll light it my own way.

Howard I don't know if I can trust you with a box of matches.

Vi Stay in then.

Howard I've got an idea. I'll make the tea now and put it in a flask.

Vi Anything not to stay in.

Howard Shall I do that for you?

Vi I don't know how your conscience will let you go out anyway, knowing I haven't had any tea.

Howard Now I asked you to have something at the same time I was having mine.

Vi I wasn't hungry then.

Howard Well, it'll have to be something quick. I've only got quarter of an hour and I haven't even shaved yet.

Vi (*contemplating*) What shall I have?

Howard Have something on toast.

Vi Oh, God, no, I'll be chasing crumbs all night. (*She moves her tongue all over her teeth*)

Howard exits to the kitchen

Howard It'll give you something to do.

Vi Cheek! (*A slight pause; she calls after him*) If there's one of them steam pies there I'll have that.

Howard (*off*) They've got to boil for thirty minutes and I haven't got the time.

Vi You can be five minutes late.

Howard (*off*) No, I can't.

Vi Five minutes isn't too much to ask.

Howard (*off*) It is if you haven't got it.

Vi You've only got to put it in a saucepan of boiling water, that's all.

Howard (*off*) I'd have to be here to open it. You know how you are with tin openers.

Vi I can't have it then?

Howard (*off*) No!

Vi Look, don't beat around the bush — give me a straight answer. You're getting hard you are. Pity I wasn't like that with you.

Howard enters from the kitchen with his battery shaver

Howard Look, am I to make a flask of tea now or not?

Vi No, leave it where it is. (*A slight pause*) If I scald myself I scald myself.

Howard (*tossing the shaver down on the chair*) If anything like that should happen, use the phone — ring.

Vi I don't know where you'll be.

Howard I didn't mean me. Ring the police. It's easy to remember: it's nine, nine, nine. (*A pause*) Look, I would leave you a number to get in touch with me, but it would only be defeating the object. You'd get me back here just to stir your bloody tea.

Vi It's at times like this I wish I'd been blessed with more children.

Howard Hey, it's at times like this I wish you'd been blessed with more.

Vi I can see what's going to be the end of me. Be found dead I will. Trying to put coal on the fire, or something like that.

Howard (*outraged but finding it funny*) You haven't put coal on the fire for over a year.

Vi That's not the point. There's a lot of things can happen to a woman when she's left in the house on her own.

Howard For three hours? Four at the most?

Vi People can die in two minutes. Especially if they've been seriously ill like me.

Howard Two minutes?

Vi A dizzy spell, a slight fall, the smallest knock on the head ...

Howard grins to himself, picks up the poker from the hearth and turns to Vi

Put that down, will you?

Howard smiles menacingly

Do you hear me? Put it down, I said.

Howard (*advancing towards Vi*) A dizzy spell, a slight fall, the smallest knock on the head.

Vi (*shouting*) Don't, Mun, you're frightening me.

Howard It's too late, you know too much.

Vi grabs for her walking stick and they begin to parry with each other. Howard screams and affects a stabbing gesture. The whole thing now resembles Norman Bates and his mother

Vi You'll give me one of my turns, and you'll have to stay in then, mind.

Howard suddenly hurts his finger and drops the poker

I don't feel safe with you any more.

Howard (*returning the poker to its original place*) I only did it for a laugh.

Vi I don't know what's got into you. That's the second time you've laughed this week.

Howard Don't you want me to be happy?

Vi Well, yes — as long as I can be happy about the same thing.

They stare at each other; a moment passes between them

Howard I'll go and see to your flask.

Howard exits

Vi Something's going on that I don't know about. (*She raises her voice a little because Howard's in the kitchen*) And I want to know what it is. (*A slight pause*) Do you hear me?

Howard (*off*) You've got nothing to worry about.

Vi Well, I will worry, and I'm not supposed to so you'd better come here now and tell me before you go out.

Howard (*off*) I haven't got time.

Vi Make time.

Howard (*off*) Don't be silly.

Vi I've noticed a difference in you this last week. I'm sitting here talking to you but your mind's off somewhere else. Very often you never quite catch what I'm saying. You're switching off, that's what you're doing. Day-dreaming. (*She raises her voice again*) And I want to know what about.

Howard enters

Howard Have you made up your mind if you're going to have something to eat?

Vi You haven't been taking any notice of me, have you?

Howard (*deliberately*) Do you want anything to eat?

Vi Yes.

Howard What?

Vi A steam pie.

Howard (*losing his patience*) You can't. I haven't got time.

Vi Excuses.

Howard (*putting his shoes on*) Have something quick. A sandwich.

Vi It's awful when children haven't got time for their own mother.

Howard Oh, please.

Vi And you still haven't cleared up that mystery.

Howard What mystery?

Vi Why you've changed from a nice boy to a laughing hyena who can't wait to get out of the house at night.

Howard You're not fair you know.

Vi (*a thought striking her*) I know what it is. You've picked up with somebody, haven't you?

Howard (*after an awkward moment*) The kettle's boiling. (*He moves towards the kitchen exit*)

Vi Hang on, wait a minute. I think you'd better come and sit down here.

Howard (*after a slight pause*) Look Mam, do me a favour — leave it for now. I haven't got time, honest. Let's talk about it again.

Vi I want to talk about it now.

Howard (*equally determined*) Well, you can't.

Vi Why not?

Howard (*shouting*) Because I don't want to talk about it.

Vi (*also shouting*) Don't you raise your voice to me.

Howard (*mimicking his mother, moving to the kitchen exit*) If your father was alive now ...

Vi If your father was alive now, he'd sort you out. He'd get to the bottom of it, right enough. You have picked up with somebody, I know you have. I can tell. Well, whoever she is, she ought to have her head examined, that's all I can say. And I don't know why it's such a big secret anyway. I'd never ask you to bring her here, so you won't have to feel ashamed of me. It's awful, isn't it? You bring them into the world, rear them up, and then they treat you like this. I was never ashamed of my mother. Never. And secrets was something we shared. All of us. When I picked up with your father I couldn't wait to show him off. He wasn't much of a catch I admit but he was mine and I was proud of him. I didn't care that he was a lot older than me — or that he was bald. It didn't matter to me. But there, I'm not you am I? Youngsters are not like they used to be. (*A slight pause. She speaks with just a little more volume*) What are you doing out there?

Howard (*off*) Making tea.

Vi (*sweetly*) Boiling me that pie are you?

Howard (*off*) No.

Vi I thought not.

Howard enters with a flask, which he places on Vi's table. There is a long pause. During the following Howard shaves in front of the mirror

I'll have a boiled egg.

Howard You're too late.

Vi You haven't got time to boil an egg?

Howard That's right.

Vi Four minutes.

Howard Sorry.

Vi All right, there then. I'll have it soft.

Howard No, you can't.

Vi And I fancy an egg, too.

Howard I haven't got time.

Vi You can be a bit late. Chances are she will be anyway.

Howard How do you know?

Vi They always are. Well, I was I know. It doesn't pay to be too early. Gives a false impression. Makes them think you're eager.

Howard I'm not eager. I'm just going to be on time. (*He finishes shaving. He takes his shirt from the back of the chair and begins to put it on*)

Vi You're not wearing that shirt?

Howard Why not?

Vi There's a black mark on it.

Howard Where?

Vi I'd show it to you, but what's the point? You haven't got time to nip upstairs and change it.

Howard (*checking the shirt*) I can't see anything. Show it to me.

Vi There's nothing wrong with it. Put it on for goodness' sake.

Howard puts on the shirt and checks himself in the mirror

(*Watching Howard*) I can forget about the egg, then?
Howard Yes.
Vi (*tutting*) I don't know why I'm sure but I'd love a couple of eggs now.
Howard (*combing his hair*) You don't give up, do you?
Vi Where's she from then?
Howard Who?
Vi This girl you've picked up with.
Howard (*after a slight pause*) You wouldn't know her.
Vi I didn't ask if I knew her, I asked you where she was from.
Howard Not around here.
Vi Do I know her?
Howard No.
Vi What's her name?
Howard (*turning to Vi*) Why?
Vi What do you mean "why"?
Howard (*reassuringly*) Look, you don't know her, right.
Vi Tell me her name then.
Howard Leave it there now, will you?
Vi What's the big secret? Something horrible is it?
Howard You're like a ferret you are. When you've got your nasty little teeth in you won't let go.
Vi (*outraged*) Fancy calling your mother a ferret.
Howard I just want you to leave it there, Mam, I don't want to talk about it.
Vi Well, that's lovely that is. (*She mocks him*) I just want you to leave it there, Mam. I don't want to talk about it. If you can't talk to your own mother, who can you talk to?
Howard Wait a minute. It's not that I can't talk to you. I don't want to.
Vi All right, don't talk about her, then.

Howard exits into the hall

Just tell me her name.
Howard (*off: shouting*) For crying out loud!
Vi Her first name, that's all. I'll be satisfied with that.

Howard returns with his jacket on

Is there anything else you want now before I go?
Vi You've always been deep you have. And if there's one thing I can't stand it's deepness. Especially in your own children. You'll be sorry one day though, because there might come a time when you'll want to talk to me and I won't be here.

Howard (*raising his voice*) Mam ... (*He sighs. He becomes much quieter now*) I don't want to talk about it because — because I'm afraid to.

Vi Afraid? What are you afraid of? Not that girl?

Howard I'm afraid of lots of things. (*He kneels next to her*) I'm afraid it might not turn out to be anything. Afraid I might say or do something and louse it up. Afraid you might never understand what I'm trying to say.

Vi Well, you're right there. I don't understand a bloody word of it.

Howard stands and moves to leave

She's not a married woman, is she?

Howard No!

Vi (*absolutely determined*) Well, Howard, you may as well know it, Howard, you're not going out of that door till you tell me her name.

Howard (*after a slight pause*) Bernice.

Vi What was that?

Howard (*after a pause*) I said, Bernice.

Vi (*after a slight pause*) Bernice? (*Incredulously*) Bernice?

Howard nods

That's her name?

Howard Yes.

Vi Never heard of her.

Howard I said you hadn't.

Vi That's a strange name.

Howard I'm off now then.

Vi Where did you say she was from?

Howard I didn't.

Vi She can't be local. Not with a name like that. What's her last name?

Howard I'm off, right?

Vi I've never heard that name before.

Howard I won't be late.

Vi What's her mother's name?

Howard Do you hear me?

Vi Her father's then?

Howard I'm going out.

Vi You've got plenty of time. That clock's ten minutes fast.

Howard I'm ready now so I may as well go.

Vi Tell me if she's local first.

Howard (*shouting*) No!

Vi No, she's not local, or not you're not going to tell me?

Howard (*beginning to crack up*) No, I'm not going to tell you.

Vi You're lying to me, I know you are. I can tell.

Howard You're not fair.

Vi I always know when you're not telling the truth.

Howard (*almost crying*) You're not bloody fair.

Vi Her name isn't Bernice, is it?

Howard (*shouting*) Yes!

Vi (*almost shouting*) Liar!

Howard Don't ruin it for me.

Vi How can I ruin it? I only want to know her name.

Howard You won't understand, I know you won't.

Vi Tell me her name.

Howard Bernice.

Vi No, it's not.

Howard It's Bernice, I tell you.

Vi You may as well say it. Come on.

Howard It's Bernice.

Vi Come on.

Howard Bernice, Bernice.

Vi Tell me.

Howard Bernice.

Vi I want the truth.

Howard (*shouting*) Bernard. It's bloody Bernard, right?

There is a terrible pause. The telephone rings for some time; eventually Howard answers it

Yes? (*He pulls himself together*) Oh, hiya, I was just leaving. (*There is a long pause as he listens to what is being said on the other end of the line*) Oh, I see. ... No, it's all right. ... No, I understand really. ... Yes, it's all right. Bye. (*He pauses, then replaces the receiver. He sighs heavily, swallows hard and looks over at his mother*) One egg or two?

The Lights fade to Black-out and remain out for the whole of the next scene. The sound of a clock ticking comes up, starting quietly and gaining in volume

SCENE 4

This scene should be pre-recorded with a stereo effect, Howard's voice coming from one speaker and Vi's from the other

During the scene, the living-room set is struck — including the carpet — and two seats are positioned to suggest a holiday coach. These can be trucked on

Vi and Howard are in bed. It is well into the night. For a moment, all we hear is the ticking of the clock

Vi (*in a loud whisper*) Howard.

There is no reply

Howard, it's me. (*Pause*) Can you hear me? (*Pause*) Howard. (*Pause*) I can't sleep. (*Pause*) Are you awake, Howard?

There is no reply

(*Shouting slowly and loudly*) Howard!
Howard (*panicking but still half asleep*) What? What's the matter?
Vi Are you sleeping?
Howard (*annoyed*) Not any more I'm not, no. What's wrong?
Vi There's nothing wrong.
Howard Then why did you wake me up?
Vi I can't sleep.
Howard Well turn over and close your eyes.
Vi I've done that. I've been turning over all night. And I'm hot. I'm like a bloody chicken on a spit in here. You don't think there's anything wrong, do you? With me, like?

There is no answer

(*Shouting*) Howard.
Howard Open your window.
Vi It is open.
Howard Open it wider then.
Vi It won't go any more. I'm sure there's something wrong.
Howard You're just excited.
Vi About going to Tenby?
Howard You're all geared up about that trip on the bus tomorrow.
Vi That's not bothering me, don't be soft. (*A slight pause*) Howard?
Howard What?
Vi Do you want to sit by the window tomorrow?
Howard (*sighing loudly*) Yes, yes.
Vi What time have we got to get up, Howard?

There is no answer

Howard, tell me what time we've got to get up in the morning.

Howard Seven o'clock.

Vi What time is it now?

Howard Twenty-five past two.

Vi Couple of hours yet then. (*A slight pause*) Four hours, is it? Or is it five?
(*A slight pause*) Is it five hours, Howard?

There is no reply

Howard, tell me how many hours it is?

Howard (*bellowing at the top of his voice*) Shut up!!!

There is a long pause

Vi (*sweetly*) Good-night, then.

The ticking continues for a few seconds followed swiftly by the ringing of the alarm clock

Jolly banjo music plays

SCENE 5

Two seats on a holiday coach

The Lights come up on Vi and Howard in the coach seats — or they are trucked on. Vi has a rather large holdall with her

The music fades, being replaced by the sounds of a coach interior

Vi rummages in the holdall

Vi They're not in here.

Howard Yes, they are — I put them there myself.

Vi Perhaps they're not in this one. Perhaps they're in one of the others.

Howard They're in with the towels and toothpaste.

Vi There's plenty of towels in here but there's not a sandwich in sight.

Howard They're there, I tell you.

Vi Did you put them in that air-tight box like I told you?

Howard I wrapped them in foil.

Vi Why didn't you put them in that air-tight box?

Howard Because it's full of Welsh cakes.

Vi Well, they'll do. Where are they? I'll have one of those.

Howard You can't. They're in the boot of the bus.

Vi I didn't see any blue case go in that boot.

Howard Yes. They're all together — now don't panic.

Vi (*after a slight pause*) What did you want to put the food in the boot for?

Howard Well, I didn't think you'd want to eat it straight away.

Vi Why keep it till we get there? The whole point was to eat it on the way.

Howard Well, if you'd helped out with some of the packing, instead of leaving it all to me, the food might have been packed all together.

Vi I'll have another feel around, but there's nothing here, I'm telling you. (*She feels around in the holdall and fishes out a foil package of sandwiches*) Is this it?

Howard Yes.

Vi Small, isn't it? Could have cut a couple more than that. I bet there's only four in there — six at the most.

Howard That's plenty. You can eat them, I'm not hungry.

Vi opens the sandwiches and bites into one

Vi (*making a face*) Cheese I asked for.

Howard We didn't have any — and I didn't have time to go out and get some.

Vi (*of the sandwich*) What's this muck?

Howard It's sandwich spread.

Vi screws up the sandwiches and foil into a small ball and throws them up the aisle of the bus

(*After a slight pause*) What did you do with those sandwiches?

Vi You said you wasn't hungry.

Howard I'm not. I just want to know what you've done with them.

Vi gestures up the aisle

You can't do that.

Vi I just have.

Howard Well, you can't.

Vi Why not? That's keeping somebody in a job, that is. When we get to Tenby somebody'll get paid a couple of bob to clean this bus out.

Howard Why don't you go to sleep?

Vi Don't be silly, I can't — not with this bag on my lap.

Howard Give it here. (*He takes the bag and rests it on his lap*) Now shut your eyes.

Vi I don't want to — I'm not tired. (*A slight pause*)

Howard Did you take those tablets this morning?

Vi What tablets?

Vi The travelling tablets.
Howard Yes.
Vi Did I?
Howard I put them out for you.
Vi I can't remember if I took them or not.
Howard Close your eyes and don't think about it.

Vi closes her eyes for a moment

Vi I don't feel very well.
Howard Close your eyes.
Vi They are closed.
Howard Relax then.
Vi I can't relax — I feel sick.
Howard Try not to think about it.

There is a pause

Vi Howard?
Howard What?
Vi Do you know what I keep thinking about?
Howard What?
Vi That sandwich spread. (*She lunges forward, retching. She presumably vomits over Howard's knees*)
Howard Oh, my God!

Black-out

SCENE 6

The caravan site

The Lights come back up. The coach sounds fade, being replaced by bird-song

Vi enters, tentatively, looking for the caravan; she carries a shoulder bag. She calls to Howard, who is off stage

Vi Found it, Howard?

There is no answer

What's this one by here? (*She reads the name of a caravan*) "The Manderley". Is it "The Manderley", Howard? (*She does not wait for an answer*) I hope it's not because if it is I'm not staying in it. Not after what happened to Joan Fontaine.

Howard (*off*) It's H15.
Vi Well, we passed H21 down there.

Howard enters, carrying several cases, bags, folding chairs and other items of luggage

Howard That was the water pressure.
Vi Put it down by here and we'll ask somebody.

Howard bends to put the items of luggage down on the floor and ends up toppling amongst them

(*Laughing*) This is the right place, is it? Don't think we're in the wrong field, do you? (*She pauses*) Hey, are you sure it said Tenby on the front of the bus and not Bournemouth?
Howard Of course it did. And you could hardly mistake the two: Tenby looks nothing like Bournemouth.
Vi How would you know? You've never been to either of them.
Howard I mean the writing on the bus. You know, the ... (*He moves his hand in a winding motion*)

Vi looks at Howard incredulously

(*Noting Vi's look*) Oh, never mind.
Vi What are you doing down there?
Howard Playing silly buggers, do you want a game? (*He gets up*) It can't be far.
Vi Did he tell you if it had a name?
Howard Who?
Vi Mr Fowler. The insurance man.
Howard Er, no. He never said, no.
Vi I'm sure it's that one there. (*She points off stage*)
Howard (*reading*) "The Manderley".
Vi That's a laugh. It looks more like your father's old pigeon cot than a mansion in the country.

Howard counts the offstage caravans, pointing at them in turn

What are you doing?
Howard Counting.
Vi If they bothered to name it, you'd think they'd take the trouble to put the number up. Am I right? Is that it?
Howard I think so.

Vi Go and have a try with the key.

Howard takes the key from Vi's shoulder bag

I'll wait for you by here.

Howard makes to leave

Just a minute. Put my chair up for me, there's a good boy?

Howard puts up a chair

I'll wait by here and keep an eye on the cases.

Howard exits

(*Calling after Howard*) Don't be long! And don't come back till you find it. (*Pause*) I hope to God it don't rain now or I don't know what I'll do. (*Pause*) I should have had him get my weekly out. God knows what bag it's in now. (*She takes a sweet out of her pocket and pops it into her mouth. She calls again*) Found it, Howard?
Howard (*off; from some distance*) This isn't it. I'll have to try further along.

There is a long pause

Vi (*quietly*) I don't know what the hell I must look like sitting by here. (*A slight pause*) I can't get over how quiet it is. (*Suddenly she reacts to seeing someone off stage* R) Ooo-hoo! (*She waves her hand to attract the person's attention*) Ooo-hoo! (*She repeats the wave*) Yes, you. Can you come here a minute? ... Yes, you. Can you—come over here—a minute? (*The person presumably makes a rude sign to her*) And the same to you, too. (*She looks away* L)

Adele, a young woman, enters L

Er, excuse me.
Adele Why, what have you done? (*She laughs hysterically*)
Vi Pardon?
Adele Don't you get it? "Why, what have you done?" "Why, what have you ...?"

Vi looks bewildered

Forget it. Taxi let you down, have they?
Vi Taxi?
Adele I shouldn't worry. Probably had a rush on. They will come sooner or later. (*A slight pause*) Enjoyed it, have you?
Vi What?
Adele The holiday?
Vi It haven't bloody started yet.
Adele Oh, I thought ... (*She laughs*) When I saw you with all your cases I thought ... (*She laughs again*) Sorry. So, you've only just arrived then?
Vi Yes, I'm waiting for my son.
Adele Oh, he'll be a while then. The men's toilets are right over the other side of the field.
Vi He hasn't gone for a pee. He's gone to look for the caravan.
Adele What number is it?
Vi H15.
Adele Oh, that's just there. (*Pointing*) Behind this one, "The Manderley".
Vi (*getting up and looking off* L) That pink thing.
Adele Yes, that's right.
Vi I thought "The Manderley" was small. That looks like a plastic pig.

Adele laughs. There is a slight pause

Adele (*moving towards Vi's luggage*) Shall I give you a hand?
Vi No, no. I'll leave it for Howard. He's my son.

Adele stops immediately. There is a slight pause

Adele I'll see you later, then. (*She heads off* R)
Vi (*calling after Adele*) You married?

Adele stops again; she finds the question very strange but answers it

Adele No.
Vi I bet you're courting though.
Adele Not at the moment.

There is a slight pause

Vi Perhaps you can give me a hand after all.

Adele picks up all of Vi's belongings during the following

It's just over there, you said. Will you be able to manage all that? I can't help you, I had a stroke last year and half of me don't work very good. (*She heads for the* L *exit*) Don't worry if you can't manage it all. You can always double back for the rest.

Vi exits in the direction of the caravan

Adele struggles across the stage with all the luggage and exits

The Lights dim

The sound of bird-song gets even louder

SCENE 7

The same. A day later

The Lights brighten to suggest sunshine and the bird-song returns to its previous level

Howard tiptoes on from behind the caravan, wearing a bathing costume and carrying a folded sun lounger, sun tan lotion, book et cetera. He moves C, still tiptoeing

Vi (*off; from the caravan*) Howard?
Howard Shit!
Vi (*off*) Where are you?
Howard I'm out here.
Vi (*off*) Come here — I want you.
Howard (*quickly putting up the lounger*) I'm busy, what do you want?
Vi (*off*) What are you doing?
Howard Putting up the sun lounger.
Vi How long are going to be out there for?
Howard I'll be a bit. Go back to sleep and I'll come in after.

There is a pause

Vi Going to read, are you?

There is no reply. Howard busies himself setting everything up

(*Shouting*) I said, you're going to read are you?
Howard Yes, I think so, yes. (*He settles down on the sun lounger, eventually taking out his book and beginning to read*)

Vi (*off*) Hey, Howard ... I can't stick this heat.
Howard Then take something off.
Vi (*off*) I can't, I'm down to my petticoat now. (*A slight pause*) I think I'll come out there with you.
Howard (*desperate for a moment alone*) It's even hotter out here.
Vi (*off*) If I was twenty years younger and two sizes smaller, I'd go topless.
Howard Stay where you are, you'll be better off indoors.
Vi (*after a slight pause*) What are you reading, Howard?
Howard Go back to sleep.
Vi Tell me what you're reading first.
Howard (*with great feeling*) "Ten Rillington Place."

Howard waits for a reaction from Vi — there isn't one. He turns and finds a more comfortable position

Vi (*shouting*) Ten where?

Howard doesn't answer her. He tosses the book to the floor in frustration and settles down to sun-bathe

Adele enters. Her pace perhaps is quite hurried until she notices Howard. She then tentatively walks around the lounger until she is standing behind him. She leans over him, casting a shadow over his face. She tickles his head playfully

Howard (*opening his eyes*) Now why didn't you stay in the caravan and have a nice quiet ... (*He realizes it's Adele and not Vi*) Oh — hiya.
Adele In the van then, is she?
Howard Having a lay down.
Adele I'm just going over the shops and I wondered if she wanted anything?
Vi (*off*) Who are you talking to, Howard?
Howard (*calling*) Adele.
Adele Only she said last night she forgot to pack the shampoo.
Howard It's all right, I fetched some this morning.
Vi (*off*) Who did you say, Howard?
Howard ⎫ (*together*) Adele.
Adele ⎭

They both laugh at saying this at the same time. There is a pause

Adele I enjoyed meself last night. It makes a change from being on me own.
Howard We play it all the time at home.
Adele I thought you looked a bit bored.

Howard No, it wasn't that. I enjoyed it as well.

Adele (*flattered*) Did you?

Howard Yeah ... I'm sorry about Mam, though.

Adele Playing Cupid, you mean? That's all right, don't worry about it.

Howard She wasn't even subtle, was she?

Adele Don't take things so serious.

Howard She went to the toilet six times. I'm really sorry.

Adele (*playing with him*) Listen Howard, do you know what your mother was really up to last night? Well, you know that deck-chair attendant? Handsome — big muscles? Well, he's got designs on your mum.

Howard (*playing along with her*) Deborah Kerr and Burt Lancaster.

Adele Passion in the surf.

Howard And free deck-chairs.

They laugh together; the laugh slowly dies away. There is a slight and awkward pause

Adele Nah, she's nice, your mum.

Howard You don't know her.

Adele Don't say that, I think she's lovely.

Howard You don't know her like I do.

Adele She thinks the world of you. (*She sits on the floor quite close to the lounger*) That's why she's trying to marry you off to some nice young girl.

Howard Well, it's a bit more complicated than that.

Adele (*after a slight pause; meaning she'd like an explanation*) Well, go on then.

Howard No, it's all right ... forget it.

They share a look; there is a slight pause

Adele She tells me you went away to college.

Howard I did for a while, yes.

Adele I sat nine CSEs.

Howard Did you? How many did you get?

Adele One.

They both laugh

And you'll never guess which one that was.

Howard shakes his head

Religious bleeding Instruction.

Howard Did you re-sit?

Adele No, I met this fella who got me a smashing job with a turf accountant. That's where I met my late husband.

Howard He was a gambler, then?

Adele No — a plumber. He turned up one day to mend the hand basin. He was a lovely looking chap; I fancied him straight away. You know the type: look good in anything, even a boiler-suit. I happened to mention that the thermostat wasn't working in my flat and he came round one day to fix it. He knew what my game was though, straight away — we didn't have central heating.

They both laugh again. They're getting on really well by this time

Howard Did you live on your own in the flat?

Adele No, I had a mate — a friend, like. We shared all the bills — and Toms — and Harrys ... And Howards.

They both laugh but Howard finds the last reference rather uncomfortable and is more than happy to move the conversation on

Howard How old were you when you left home?

Adele Sixteen.

Howard (*amazed*) And your mother let you go?

Adele Let me go? She threw me out. We never got on — not since I was a baby. Not since the time I threw up all over the vicar at her wedding. (*She laughs*)

Howard laughs too

No, that wasn't true. All the same — we never got on. Never had a good relationship — not like you've got with your mother.

Howard Can you imagine her letting me leave home?

Adele Do you want to?

Howard I've got to.

Adele Why don't you then?

Howard It's not easy, not the way things are.

Adele Have you talked to her about it?

Howard I've hinted a bit.

Adele Well, that's not good enough. Tackle her on it. Tell her how you feel. She's your mother — I'm sure she's not totally insensitive to your feelings.

Howard Well, like I said — you don't know her.

Adele Bit like the old ball and chain, is she then?

Howard You wouldn't believe it.

Adele I can understand though, you know — to a certain extent.

Howard (*surprised*) Can you?

Adele Well, it's her husband innit? Your father. She wouldn't be clinging so much if he were still alive. She's hanging on to you, luvvie, because you're all she's got.

Howard But I feel I've done my bit.

Adele And so you have, I'm sure—and done it well too, I imagine. Too well, if you know what I mean.

Howard looks at Adele

You see, you've lulled her, ain't you? Into a false sense of security. You've made her feel so comfortable with you she's probably afraid of facing the possibility of you not being there.

Howard Yes, that's right.

Adele What you have to do is somehow build her confidence back up. Get her to do things for herself, you know what I mean?

Howard I'm trying.

Adele She's got to get more independent or you don't stand a chance.

Howard I keep telling her to make new friends.

Adele That's right. Get her to enjoy herself without you.

There is a slight pause. In their enthusiasm they find themselves physically very close to each other. After a moment, Adele breaks away

Anyway, I've got to go. (*She heads towards the R exit*)

Howard You're very good, you know. You should have sat psychology.

Adele Yeah, I know. I'd have got a degree in mothers.

Adele exits R

Black-out

Some very loud heavy metal music plays

SCENE 8

A telephone box

There is a municipal waste-paper bin in front of the Tenby flat

The Lights come up; the music fades

Howard is in the telephone box and in the middle of a call. A young girl is waiting; she has a pair of rollers on her feet and is listening to a personal stereo. She skates round the area while waiting for Howard to finish

Howard (*into the phone; in answer to "How is it down there?"*) All right — it's OK. ... Well, I might not be able to speak for long. ... No, it's my mother. ...No, I've left her on the prom. I sat her down by an old gent with gout and told her I had to pay a call. ... When are you coming down? I'm going crazy. Yeah, Thursday's all right. ... Don't worry, I'll get away somehow, even if I've got to stick her in a boat and send her to Caldy Island. ... Great. ... The afternoon is better, it'll give me the morning to arrange something.

Vi enters carrying two melting ice-cream cornets. She is obviously looking for Howard

No, I haven't.
Vi (*to the girl on skates*) Don't know where the men's toilets are, do you love?
Howard (*into the phone*) I've hinted a bit.
Vi (*to the girl*) It's not for me — I don't want the men's toilets. I'm looking for my son. About five-foot-six — thin — dark hair.
Howard (*into the phone*) Of course, it'll be all right. Don't worry about it.
Vi (*to the girl*) I won't be five minutes, he said.
Howard (*into the phone*) It'll work out — you wait and see.
Vi (*to the girl*) Five minutes! He's been gone half an hour already.
Howard (*into the phone*) I will tell her, but I'm going to have to choose my moment.
Vi (*to the girl*) Where's the ice-cream parlour? I wouldn't mind betting he's buggered off for a peach melba.
Howard (*into the phone*) I have tried talking to her about it but each time she just switches off. It's not going to be easy.
Vi (*to the girl*) Don't fancy a cornet, do you? These are melting all over my fingers.
Howard (*into the phone*) Where shall we meet on Thursday, then?
Vi (*to the girl*) Eighty pence each these are. Dear, i'n' they?
Howard (*into the phone*) Yeah, I don't mind, we can have a peach melba then.
Vi (*to the girl*) Local girl, are you? Or are you down here on holidays?
Howard (*into the phone*) Half-past one, then.
Vi (*to the girl*) I don't know if I'd like to live by the sea-side, myself. I'm not sure I'd like all those foreigners invading the place in the summer. Your home's not your own then, somehow, is it? Take him by there now — (*she*

faces the phone box) I lay any odds he's a holiday-maker, phoning home
to a —— (*She spots Howard*)

Howard sees Vi at the same moment

Howard (*into the phone*) Oh, God — she's found me!
Vi What are you doing in there, Howard?
Howard (*into the phone*) Look — I'm going to have to go. (*He hangs up
  the phone*)
Vi (*to the girl*) That's him! That's my boy. Howard! What are you doing in
  there?
Howard Picking cockles—what the hell do you think I'm doing? (*He moves
  away* DR)

*The girl picks up the receiver and remains on the phone until the end of the
scene*

Vi (*following him*) Who do you know with a phone?
Howard Bernard.
Vi (*she stops, pauses, then advances again*) What did you want to leave me
  by that smelly old man for?
Howard He was the only one on there.
Vi I'm sure he hadn't changed his socks for six months. If you don't want
  me hanging round you, why did you bring me on holiday?
Howard It's not that I don't want you hanging round me. It's just that I need
  some space sometimes. Room to live.
Vi If it's more space you want, you should have hired a bigger caravan.
Howard That's not what I mean, and you know it.

Vi hands Howard his cornet

Vi It's not fair to bring me on holidays if you don't want to be with me.
Howard I do want to be with you — but not all the time. You've got to let
  me go a little bit.
Vi (*after a pause*) That's him, innit?
Howard Who?
Vi That Bernard, whoever he is. He's making you talk like this.
Howard Don't be silly.
Vi I'm right, I don't care what you say.
Howard You can't blame him for something I did.
Vi You did? What do you mean? What have you done?
Howard I've let you crowd me, corner me, and it's not fair. Not to you or
  me.

Vi What has he said to you on that phone?

Howard (*moving away* UR) Why?

Vi Well, he must have said something to start you off like this. Ooh, I've got no time for people like that.

Howard (*on the attack*) Like what?

Vi Like ... you know.

Howard (*coming back* DS, *standing on Vi's* L) Homosexual?

Vi Shhh!

Howard You've got time for me.

Vi (*shouting*) You are not — (*she mouths the word*) homosexual.

Howard (*insisting*) I've told you, I am.

Vi (*insisting even more*) Well, you're not! I won't have it. You're just a bit confused, that's all. (*A slight pause*) Your father had a cousin who was ...

Howard Homosexual?

Vi reluctantly nods

Who is he?

Vi You wouldn't know him. None of the family bothered with him once they found out. He moved away in the end. Best thing to do. He's dead now. He wasn't very old either. But there, they all die young.

Howard Who do?

Vi Men like that.

Howard Don't talk rubbish.

Vi They do. They lose all control of their (*she mouths the word*) bowels, and they die. I read it in the *Sun*.

There is a pause between them

Do I really?

Howard What?

Vi Crowd you.

Howard Yes.

Vi Why didn't you tell me before?

Howard I didn't really realize until ——

Vi Bernard.

Howard Look, it's not that he said anything. It's just that I'm not helping you by always being there — and I do think you could do more now. If you tried a bit harder you could have a life of your own — and so could I ... but there's no reason why we shouldn't share part of it.

Vi (*after a slight pause; quietly*) You want to go — don't you?

Howard It's not that I want to go. Well, yes, it is that I want to go but I wouldn't just leave ... You're my mother, I love you — and I wouldn't do that.

Vi (*vulnerable*) I can't manage on my own.

Howard Of course you can. Look, we can't talk about it here — let's go back to the caravan.

Vi But you've always been there.

Howard Come on; we won't walk, we'll catch a bus.

Vi Who'll make me breakfast in the mornings?

Howard You will.

Vi How will I use the tin opener?

Howard There are gadgets.

Vi Who will I talk to?

Howard I'll phone you.

Vi Not every day. I won't see a face from one week to the next — except perhaps the insurance man. And who'll get my tablets for me?

Howard There'll be a warden. Everything can be sorted out. Come on, let's go.

Vi (*snapping*) No, I'm not.

Howard Oh, don't be like that.

Vi You'd better go on your own. That way you can have room to live all the way back to the caravan.

Howard Please?

Vi Why can't you go on your own?

Howard Because you don't know the way.

Vi Well, I can ask, can't I? I've still got a tongue in my mouth.

Howard Don't spoil it now, Mam.

Vi What?

Howard This holiday.

Vi How can you spoil something that's already been ruined?

Howard (*a slight pause*) Come on, let's get some cod and chips and take them back to the van.

Vi (*almost shouting*) Don't think you can tempt me with a piece of cod, because you can't!

There is a slight pause. Howard moves up behind Vi

Howard Hake then?

Vi (*not thinking about it for too long*) Oooh, all right. You know exactly what to do to get the better of me. (*She heads for the exit* L) I'm not paying, mind. This is your treat not mine. And it's still not over — this business with you. All I've done is agree to talk about it over fish and chips. (*She turns towards Howard*) Well, come on Howard, or there'll be bugger all left.

Music plays, possibly "Beanfields" by the Penguin Café Orchestra

Howard tosses his ice-cream into the bin. The Lights fade to Black-out

The caravan interior is set up or trucked on

SCENE 9

Inside the caravan. Half an hour or so later

The music fades and the Lights come up dimly, suggesting a caravan interior

Howard and Vi are eating their fish and chips out of newspaper

Vi Nicer in paper, i'n' they?
Howard And I'd set everything up before I went.
Vi Your father was the boy for fish and chips.
Howard And of course I'd wait until you were completely settled in first.
Vi He'd eat 'em until they were coming out of his ears. Course that was in the days when fish and chips was cheap.
Howard You haven't listened to anything, have you?
Vi Eh?

Howard, exasperated, runs his fingers through his hair

Don't do that, Howard, your hair's greasy enough as it is.
Howard You said we could talk.
Vi We are talking.
Howard About me.
Vi We haven't stopped talking about anyone else.
Howard (*firmly*) I want to talk about me and you.
Vi (*after a slight pause*) Go on then. (*She rams more chips into her mouth*)
Howard You must try and understand how I feel.
Vi I do understand. You want a place of your own.
Howard Yes.
Vi Somewhere where you can come and go as you please.
Howard That's right.
Vi And not to have to answer to anyone. To be free and be your own boss.
Howard But just because I want all those things, it doesn't mean I don't care about you.
Vi Of course it doesn't. You'll still want to know how I am, and if I'm taking my tablets and so on.
Howard And if you're doing your exercises and making new friends. We can arrange to phone each other every other day. We can keep in touch that way.

Vi We can do better than that. We'll turn the front room into a bed-sitter. I can go in there and you can have the run of the rest of the house.

Howard (*shouting*) No!

Vi But we can do all we want that way and you can still be your own boss.

Howard I'll never be in charge of me as long as we're under the same roof.

Vi Well, that's lovely that is. So you don't think you're in charge?

Howard doesn't answer

Who does all the shopping and housework then? Sees to all the business?

Howard In charge of me, I said. You know perfectly well I didn't mean those sort of things.

Vi (*after a pause*) If you go, it will be with that Bernard, I suppose.

Howard I thought I may go back to college — finish my degree.

Vi So that's what it is.

Howard What?

Vi Why you're like you are with me. You blame me for dragging you out of college and making you come back here to look after me.

Howard You didn't drag me out of anywhere. When you had your stroke, I came back here to look after you because I wanted to. No-one made me do anything. You needed me then.

Vi I need you now.

Howard No — you don't! I'm not helping you any more. You're relying on me and you shouldn't. If you are going to conquer this thing you are going to have to do it on your own.

Vi That's not what you told me in hospital. "It's all right," you said, "I'm here now and we'll beat it together."

Howard In the beginning I did things because you couldn't. Now I do them because you won't. If I wasn't here you'd have to fend for yourself and that would be good for you.

Vi I see. So you only want to go away for my sake?

Howard No, it's for me too. But it's not all for me.

Vi It isn't?

Howard No!

Vi So when I'm sitting by the fire, freezing because I can't put the coal on, and dying of thirst because I can't handle the cooker, it will all be for my own good?

Howard (*after a pause*) It should be the other way about. You should want me to go. I should be going under protest. Going, wondering if I'm doing the right thing.

Vi I reckon if you go, you'll go like that anyway.

Howard (*after a slight pause*) It's not fair, you know me too well.

Vi I should, I've lived with you long enough.

Howard Don't you ever get fed up of me? Don't you sometimes wish I'd bugger off out and leave you alone? If only for a couple of hours?

Vi No, never. (*She touches his arm*) You're all I've got.

Howard (*putting his hand on top of hers*) You're all I've got, too ——

Vi (*snatching her hand back*) No, I'm not. You've got some bugger else now.

Howard I haven't got anyone — except you.

Vi And you don't bloody want me. (*A slight pause*) If you haven't got anyone else — where does this Bernard fit into it then?

Howard He's — someone I can talk to. Impartial, unprejudiced. He helps me think — helps me see myself.

Vi (*after a slight pause*) So, he's just a friend then?

Howard (*after a pause*) Look, in the same way I had to come back, I've got to go ... I've got to go.

Vi If something should happen to me ...

Howard Nothing is going to happen to you.

Vi What will I do with myself when you are not here?

Howard The same as you did for the first two years I was at college.

Vi I was working then.

Howard Well, go back to it.

Vi Talk sense, will you?

Howard I'm serious. There's no reason why you shouldn't go back to the "Plaza".

Vi I can't usherette now.

Howard Why not?

Vi How will I hold the torch?

Howard In your other hand.

Vi And what do you suggest I rip the tickets with — my teeth?

Howard I'm sure you'll manage.

Vi You're talking nonsense — I'll never work again. Anyway, they wouldn't take me back.

Howard You're not going to know until you ask.

Vi You're not pushing me back to work, Howard, and that's an end to it.

Howard I'm not trying to push you anywhere. I'm just trying to help you.

Vi Why don't you find a job?

Howard No-one is going to employ me until I get my degree.

Vi Do something else. You haven't got to teach.

Howard But I want to.

Vi Well, we all got to do things we don't want to sometimes.

Howard And that includes you.

Vi It's not a case of not wanting to go back to work. I'm not a well woman.

Howard You're fine now.

Vi No. All that sort of thing is out for me.

Howard (*absolutely determined*) Well, whether you take a job or not, it's of no difference. I've made up my mind and I'm going.

Vi (*after a slight pause*) So, you've already decided then?

Howard Yes.

Vi Can I ask when?

Howard Just now. I decided just now.

Vi It doesn't sound like just now to me.

Howard I've been thinking about it for a while.

Vi Ever since you met this Bernard.

Howard Yes ... no!

Vi He's definitely got something to do with it, Howard. I don't care what you say. Does he know you live at home with your mother?

Howard Of course he does.

Vi I bet you haven't told him you look after me because I've had a stroke though.

Howard He knows all about your stroke.

Vi And he's still told you to go away and leave me?

Howard He hasn't told me to do anything.

Vi I bet his own mother's dead. If she was alive, he wouldn't have this sort of attitude.

Howard He's not like you think at all.

Vi Is his mother dead, Howard?

Howard He only wants what's best for me.

Vi (*shouting*) Is his mother dead?

Howard (*shouting back*) Yes!

Vi (*still with raised voice*) There you are, I knew — didn't I tell you? Perhaps I'd better talk to this Bernard, so's I can put him straight.

Howard You wouldn't do that.

Vi Wouldn't I?

Howard You're not that selfish.

Vi (*her engine still running*) Since when is it selfish to want to be taken care of? Only one son I've got — and one mother you'll have too, my boy, so if I were you, I'd think again.

Howard (*determinedly*) I have thought and I'm going.

Vi (*an outburst*) If you do, I'll take tablets.

Howard (*becoming emotional*) That's not fair.

Vi I will — I'll take a whole bottle.

Howard You can't blackmail me.

Vi I just have. And I mean it, I'll take every bloody tablet in the house.

Howard (*shouting and crying*) Take them then. Take them and see if I bloody care!

Howard storms out of the caravan and off

Vi (*after Howard has left*) Howard? I know you're out there. Come back in here, please, I want you. Howard!

There is no reply

Howard, I want you, I said. (*She now begins to believe he isn't there and she has been left on her own. Her next call is of a completely different tone*) Howard?

Violin music plays, very quietly, as at the beginning of the play

Black-out

ACT II

Scene 1

An open area away from the caravans. There is a tap here, and makeshift washing lines with pegs

Violin music plays. The Lights come up

Adele is pegging some skimpy underwear on one of the lines

Vi enters with Howard's swimming things — bathers and towel, et cetera. She hangs them on a line directly opposite Adele

Vi Hot, innit?

Adele Oh, you're back then?

Vi Just now. Couldn't stick it any longer.

Adele Where'd you go?

Vi Only down the beach. Howard wanted a dip. Sand was so hot it was burning your feet.

Adele I came over earlier but I could see you were out.

Vi Must have gone about ten.

Adele (*after a slight pause*) Everything all right?

Vi No, I'm too hot.

Adele I mean with you and Howard.

Vi (*after a slight pause*) Why are you asking?

Adele I passed on my way to the loo last night.

Vi (*horrified — but only for the briefest of moments*) Couldn't hear us, could you?

Adele (*laughing*) I should think the whole bleedin' site heard you.

Vi (*laughing as well*) Fancy. You forget you're in a caravan, don't you? I can shout at him as loud as I like back home, houses are built like a fortress.

Adele All patched up now, is it?

Vi (*playing the martyr*) He left me for over an hour.

Adele I'm not surprised. It sounded as though you both needed to cool off.

Vi I didn't think he'd leave me for as long as that. I started to wonder at one time if he'd left me on my own altogether.

Adele Gone back home, you mean?

Vi The way he's been acting lately he's quite capable of doing that.

Adele I don't think he would have somehow.

Vi Nothing would surprise me. (*She takes Adele into her confidence*) Between you and me, he's got it in his head to go back to college.

Adele Good.

Vi (*surprised*) What?

Adele Well, you want him to get on, don't you?

Vi Yes, but ... Well, there's me, i'n' there.

Adele What about you?

Vi Well, he can't, can he? Not now I'm like this. (*She points to her arm*)

Adele Oh, your stroke, you mean.

Vi Well, of course.

Adele Oh ... I didn't realize you were an invalid.

Vi (*not liking the sound of that word*) I'm not.

Adele Handicapped, then.

Vi (*disliking that one even more*) I'm not that either.

Adele Oh, I'm glad. They're not nice labels, are they? (*A pause*) What is it then?

Vi What?

Adele Your label. What pigeon-hole do you fit in?

Vi Pigeon-hole?

Adele If you're not handicapped or an invalid, what do you class yourself as?

Vi (*think for a moment*) I suppose I'm slightly ... partially ...

Adele (*laughing*) What does that mean?

Vi A bit of both, innit.

There is a slight pause. Adele wrings out a pair of knickers at the drain

Adele It's none of my business, of course, but I think he's getting a bit of a raw deal meself.

Vi Who?

Adele Howard.

Vi (*a little put out*) Oh?

Adele At least that's the way it looks to me — and others too, I imagine.

Vi Others?

Adele Yes, you know, the people down the street, women in the shops. I bet they all think it's a bit sad really. I know I did.

Vi What's sad?

Adele Well, he told me he was doing very well in college. It seems such a shame he had to give it all up.

Vi He didn't have to. He wanted to. He told me that last night.

Adele Oh, well, there you are then — as long as he wanted to.

Vi He did ... Yes ... He did.

Adele (*pegging the knickers on the line*) I have to be honest, it's you I feel a bit sorry for.

Vi Me?

Adele You know how people are. The gossip. I mean I know of course that if you had anything to do with it, you'd let him go, wouldn't you?

Vi (*after a slight pause; with a hundred per cent commitment*) I would ... yes.

Adele It's the other people, the ignorant ones, the ones that don't know; it's them that's going to think the worst.

Vi (*a little worried now*) Worst?

Adele They'll blame it on you. They'll think it's you that's put a stop to it. And there's nothing worse than gossip, is there? Still, as long as you know, that's the main thing.

Vi (*in a bit of a spot*) It's getting hotter.

Adele Haven't you got a nice sun-dress? Something without sleeves and a lower neck perhaps.

Vi (*looking for someone to blame*) Those colleges are half the trouble. Sharing flats with gangs of other boys.

Adele There's nothing wrong in that, Vi love.

Vi Anything goes in them places. He'd have been better off getting into Cardiff and travelling down every day.

Adele I shared a flat and I behaved myself.

Vi Yes, but boys are different to girls.

Adele (*laughing again*) I should think they are, Vi, yes.

Vi (*joining Adele at the drain; confidentially*) He's got a friend.

Adele I bet he's got lots of friends.

Vi No, I mean one in particular.

Adele A best friend?

Vi (*reluctantly*) A bit more than that.

Adele (*after a slight pause; looking directly at Vi*) You mean a gay friend?

Vi Well, I suppose he's happy — I don't know, I've never met him.

Adele (*smiling*) Queer. Homosexual.

Vi Yes, that's right — one of them.

Adele Well, there's nothing wrong in that, Vi. I know lots of people like that. It doesn't mean to say Howard is.

Vi Well, he is — he told me.

Adele (*really disappointed, but then tossing it aside*) So, he's out.

Vi Out?

Adele What about his friend?

Vi What about him?

Adele Is he out of the closet as well?

Vi What closet?

Adele Have you talked to him?

Vi I don't know him. I only know his name.

Adele I think you two ought to get together, or the three of you is even better. I know it's not easy to accept at first, but it's not such a terrible thing these days.

Vi It is where I live.

Adele Look, when you get back home after your holiday find out if he's out of the closet or not.

Vi looks vaguely at Adele

If he admits it — if he can talk, you know, if he can talk — well, talk. It's the only thing to do. (*A pause*) Hey, Vi, fancy coming into town tomorrow? (*She moves up the line, touching each piece of washing as she goes*) I know a shop that'll have a sun-dress for you. Eh?

Vi I promised Howard I'd go back down the beach tomorrow morning.

Adele Well, that's all right, I'm busy till the afternoon.

Vi It's Thursday tomorrow. Won't it be shut half-day?

Adele No, not in Tenby. See you later.

Adele exits

Vi is left to ponder at the tap

The Lights fade to Black-out. Music plays; "California Girls" by the Beach Boys

SCENE 2

On the beach

The music fades and is replaced by beach sounds — people, the sea, birds et cetera. The Lights come up

Vi and Howard enter. Vi is carrying her handbag; Howard has a deck-chair, air-bed and bag with towels, a flask of tea, cups et cetera

Vi By here will do. Shall we stay by here?

Howard (*slightly cooler towards her than before*) If you like.

Vi Perhaps by the wall is better.

Howard Make up your mind.
Vi Which would you rather?
Howard I'm not bothered.
Vi Perhaps there's more room up by the wall.
Howard Perhaps there's not either.
Vi Best stay here, then.

Howard moves to dump everything in the sand

(*Stopping him*) Unless we go over there, look. (*She points*) That looks like a nice spot. (*She looks at Howard*)

Howard drops everything where he stands

(*Looking at the fallen objects, then at Howard*) We'll stay here, then.

Howard sits

Lots of people, Howard. I fancy there's more here than yesterday.

Howard begins to blow up the air-bed

Put my chair up, there's a good boy.
Howard You can do that.
Vi But I ——
Howard I'm blowing this up a minute. Have a go yourself.
Vi Are you still funny to me?

Howard doesn't answer but continues to blow up the bed. Vi has problems with the deck-chair. After some time she still hasn't erected it

Have a rest a minute or you'll be fainting.

Howard stops

I'm not having much luck with this.
Howard You can do it, go on.
Vi I should have had you bring my other one. I never could put up a deck-chair, even with two hands.
Howard You've about got it now. (*He points*) Just lift that end up.

Vi does as instructed and the chair is erected

There you are. See what you can do when you try?

Vi I couldn't have done it if you hadn't told me how.

Howard returns to the air-bed

(*Sitting tentatively*) I hope to God this is safe, now, Howard. (*She makes herself comfortable and looks out, as if at the sea*) The sea's a long way out. You're sure you'll be all right now this afternoon?

Howard Yes.

Vi I don't like the thought of leaving you on your own.

Howard I'll enjoy it.

Vi I don't really want to go. I'm sorry I said yes now.

Howard You can't let her down.

Vi No, I know that. What will you do then?

Howard I'll be all right on my own. You shouldn't worry about me.

Vi But I do. I'll worry where you are and what you're doing.

Howard I've told you where I'll be, I'll be in the caravan.

Vi We shouldn't be long anyway — couple of hours, that's all.

Howard You haven't got to rush.

Vi I just wish you had some company, that's all. (*She looks out, towards the* L *of the audience*) Hey, Howard, look at the shape on her.

Howard looks to the same spot and they both laugh. There is a slight pause

You'll rest then, will you, when I'm gone?

Howard I expect so.

Vi If I was that size, I'd never go in a bathing suit.

Howard You are that size.

Vi I'm not as big as her.

Howard You're the same shape.

Vi (*after a slight pause, looking over in the same direction*) I'm sure that's not her husband. (*She looks a little harder*) She's got a wedding ring on though. (*She studies the distant family*) She just asked him how much sugar he takes — well, if they were married, she'd know, wouldn't she?

Howard Not if they were newly-weds.

Vi Down here on honeymoon, you mean?

Howard Why not?

Vi No, can't be — she's got two kids with her.

Howard It can't be her fancy-man then, can it? Not if she's brought the kids with her.

Vi No, you're right. (*She gives the offstage characters one long last look*) I wonder who he is. (*There is a slight pause, then she gives up on them*) Did we bring anything to eat?

Howard In the bag. (*He moves the bag nearer her with his foot and continues to blow up the sun-bed*)

Vi I don't want anything, I was just checking. Hurry up and finish with that thing.

Howard I've done it now. (*He lays the airbed down and takes off his T-shirt. He does not yet relax on to the airbed*) Now, look: I don't mind you talking to me, right? You can say what you like — as long as it doesn't require an answer. OK?

Vi (*a little reluctant*) OK.

Howard lies down. There is a pause. Vi puts on her sunglasses. Suddenly she spots something further away on the beach. Her head moves from side to side, echoing the movement of a frisbee being thrown between two people

What are those things, Howard? (*She realizes that that was a question*) Sorry. (*There is a slight pause; she continues to watch, head still moving*) Trying to figure out I am, what those two young boys are throwing at each other. Looks a bit like a flying saucer.

Howard (*mumbling*) Frisbee.

Vi (*laughing*) No — it's nothing like a trilby, it's flat, like a plate.

Howard (*raising his voice a little*) It's a frisbee. It's a bit like a boomerang.

Vi (*still watching the frisbee*) Is that all they do then? Throw it to each other all the time?

Howard doesn't answer. He closes his eyes

(*Following the action, looking like a spectator in a tennis match*) And if it's like a boomerang, shouldn't it keep coming back? (*There is no reply*) Howard? (*She looks at Howard. A moment passes. She takes off her glasses*) Howard, I've been thinking. About this Bernard.

Howard moves his head slightly

Perhaps when we get back home, I should meet him.

Howard raises himself up on to one elbow

Not to make a row; nothing like that. Just to talk. The three of us. Shall we do that, Howard? Do you think he can talk about it? (*She looks straight at him*) What I mean is: is he out of the ottoman?

There is a pause. Howard begins to laugh. It develops into a hearty laugh

The general noise of the beach gets louder, drowning Howard out. The Lights fade to Black-out but almost immediately come back up

The scene continues but some time has passed. Howard is now lying on his stomach. Vi is dozing. After a moment, she awakes. She is a bit stiff and gets up to stretch herself. She looks around the beach and suddenly does a double-take; she has spotted someone off L

Vi Howard? Howard, you're not going to believe this. Ooh! Ooh! (*She tries to get the attention of the offstage person*) Howard, look who it is, Howard. (*She hits Howard's leg*) Wake up.
Howard (*groggily*) What's the matter?
Vi Look who's down there.
Howard Where?
Vi There, look.
Howard What time is it? (*He looks for his watch in the bag*)
Vi Down there, standing in front of that woman who's having a baby.
Howard (*panicking*) It's twenty-five past one.
Vi It's Mr Fowler.
Howard Who?
Vi Mr Fowler. The insurance man.
Howard (*getting up to look*) Where?
Vi There, look. (*She points*) With the snorkel and the flippers. (*She calls again*) Ooh! Ooh! (*She waves*) Why is he ignoring us, Howard?
Howard He probably can't see us.
Vi I can see him. (*She calls again*) Ooh! Ooh! (*She waves again*) There you are, he can see us now, he's waving back.
Howard Are you sure?
Vi Yes. I recognized him straight away. (*She mouths largely so that the offstage Bernard can lip-read her*) Know us now? Mrs Davies. (*She points to herself*) And Howard.

Vi grabs Howard by the arm and positions him in Bernard's sight-line

Wave to the insurance man, Howard.

Howard sighs heavily

Go on, wave!

Howard reluctantly waves

I wonder if he'll come over. (*She waves her good arm about, almost hitting Howard*)
Howard What are you doing?
Vi I'm calling him over. He looks as if he's on his own.

Howard Perhaps he wants to be by himself. Leave him where he is.
Vi Not everybody's like you. Here he comes.

Vi beams towards Bernard L. *Howard doesn't look so pleased*

> *Bernard enters* L. *He is still wet from the sea and is wearing flippers and has the goggles and snorkel on his head*

Hallo, Mr Fowler. Nice to see you.
Bernard Mrs Davies. Howard.

Howard smiles nervously

Vi On your own, are you?
Bernard That's right.
Vi Come and sit by us if you like. Howard was just going to pour a flask of tea.
Bernard Oh, I don't want to intrude.
Vi Nonsense. Go and get your things and bring them over by here.
Bernard Well, if you're sure.
Howard Perhaps Mr Fowler has got to go somewhere. (*To Bernard*) Have you?
Bernard (*not sure what to say*) Well, er ——
Vi (*to Howard*) There you are see, he hasn't. (*To Mr Fowler*) Hurry up with your things now and Howard will pour the tea by the time you come back.
Bernard Right.

> *Bernard exits*

Howard What did you want to invite him over here for?
Vi Pity to see him on his own. Pour the tea, go on.
Howard (*opening the flask and pouring tea during the following*) I only brought two cups.
Vi Give him the top of the flask, it'll be all right. (*She sits back in the deckchair*) Fancy recognizing him among all these people.
Howard Fancy.
Vi I could see it was him, even with his snorkel on. Funny how he never said anything about coming down.
Howard Perhaps he just decided on the spur of the moment.
Vi You don't think he's down here to keep an eye on his caravan, do you?
Howard I shouldn't think so.
Vi Whatever you do, say nothing about that milk jug I smashed.
Howard I won't — or the sugar bowl.

Vi I'd better replace them today. (*A slight pause*) I wonder if he's doing anything this afternoon.

Howard Why?

Vi He could be company for you while I'm out shopping.

Howard He's probably got his day planned. I'm sure he doesn't want to spend it hanging around us.

Vi Perhaps he's at a bit of a loose end. He might jump at the chance of spending some time with us.

Bernard enters carrying his clothes, a towel, et cetera

(*To Bernard*) I was just saying to Howard, now, Mr Fowler: perhaps you'd like to come back to the caravan. Have some tea with us later on. I'm going shopping with Adele, that's a friend I've made on the site. Maybe you'd keep an eye on Howard for me while I'm gone.

Howard (*scornfully*) Mam!

Bernard (*very unsure*) Tea would be very nice. Yes. (*He looks at Howard*)

Howard sighs and looks away

Vi Right, that's settled then. How are you getting on, Howard?

Howard hands Vi a cup of tea

Ta. It's one sugar for Mr Fowler.

Howard I know. (*He offers Bernard a cup of tea*)

Bernard Can you hang on to it a minute? I think I'll get dressed first.

Fowler begins to dry himself with the towel, wiping himself in the crotch area

Vi (*to Bernard*) Wipe dry now — you don't want to catch pneumonia.

Howard looks at Vi, annoyed. Bernard continues to dry himself off

Is it nice in?

Bernard Pardon?

Vi The water.

Bernard Oh, yes — it's lovely.

Vi Didn't know you liked diving.

Bernard Have a go at anything, that's me.

Bernard and Howard share a fleeting glance

Vi Down for the day, is it?

Bernard Yes, back home tonight.
Vi Don't suppose it's far in the car?
Bernard Couple of hours.
Vi Took us four hours on the bus, didn't it, Howard?

Howard just nods, sipping his tea

That's the only thing that's putting me off this holiday, it's the thought of
travelling all that way back. Pity you hadn't come down on Saturday, we
could have had a lift home with you then.

Howard almost chokes

Bernard I could do that if you liked.
Howard What?
Bernard Make a trip down on Saturday.

*During the following, Bernard finishes drying himself, wraps the towel round
his waist and tries to remove his swimming trunks — without much success
initially*

Vi That would be nice, Howard.
Howard Don't be silly — Mr Fowler couldn't do that.
Vi He just said he could.
Howard We've got return tickets, remember?
Vi Yes, I know, but travelling all that way — and I don't travel very good.
Remember what happened on the way here? (*To Bernard*) I was bad all
over his lap. (*To Howard*) It's not nice to refuse a lift, Howard, not after Mr
Fowler has been so good as to offer. (*To Bernard*) Thank you very much,
Mr Fowler, we'd love a lift on Saturday. (*She gives Howard a rotten look.
To Bernard*) Having trouble?
Bernard I think I'll manage. (*He tries holding the towel with his teeth*)
Vi Go on ... you're in a hell of a mess.

Bernard almost drops the towel

Give Mr Fowler a hand, Howard.
Howard What can I do?
Vi Go and hold the towel for him.
Howard I'm sure he can manage.
Vi The last thing I want is for that towel to fall. Go and hold it for him I said.

Howard still doesn't move

If Mr Fowler exposes himself, it'll be your fault.

Howard stands and reluctantly holds the towel for Bernard; however Bernard still has problems putting on his underpants, putting both legs into the same hole and finding it difficult to keep his balance, et cetera. Vi watches all of this, laughing and smiling to herself. Eventually, Bernard succeeds with the underpants

Been down here long?

Bernard Since about eleven. (*He puts on his trousers during the following*)

Vi It's warmed up a lot now. I'm going to buy a sun-dress this afternoon. I'll be a bit cooler then.

Bernard Have you enjoyed yourself?

Vi Yes, we have, haven't we, Howard?

Howard It's been OK, yeah.

Bernard Caravan all right for you?

Vi A bit small but we've managed. Saw the sign in the kitchen.

Bernard I had to put one up. Every time I let the van out, someone either broke the milk jug or the sugar bowl.

Vi looks at Howard and covers a smile

Vi (*to Howard; mouthing*) Shut your mouth. (*To Bernard*) I bet you come down regular in the summer, do you?

Bernard I have to if I let the van.

Vi See people in and out and so on.

Bernard That's right.

Vi There you are, see Howard, he would have had to have come down on Saturday anyway. (*She gets her camera from her bag and aims it at Bernard and Howard*) Smile. (*She takes a photograph*)

As Vi takes the photograph, Howard lets the towel go — but Bernard has more or less got his trousers on by this time

Black-out. The beach noises fade

SCENE 3

This scene alternates between a shopping centre and the beach at Tenby, and ends outside the caravan

Street sounds can be heard. The Lights come up

Vi and Adele are shopping

Vi And there he was as large as life standing not twenty yards away. You will
come round after now, won't you? Have some tea and meet him?
Adele Yeah, course I will.
Vi We left him on the pier. He wouldn't come back with us this time, he said
he had to take some things back to his car. Howard's gone back to meet him
by half-past two. (*She nods to something in an imaginary shop window*)
That's nice, isn't it?
Adele You don't like that?
Vi I like the colour.
Adele You don't want anything with sleeves. Come on, let's go further
along.

They exit DR

*Black-out. The street sounds give way to the call of seagulls. The Lights come
up*

   Bernard is standing DL

Howard approaches excitedly from UC *and rushes over to Bernard*

Howard Hiya!

Bernard makes a face and crosses in front of Howard

   What's the matter?
Bernard You haven't told her.
Howard Yes, I have. She knows I want to leave.
Bernard You haven't told her who I am.
Howard Not yet — but I will though.
Bernard (*lightening up a bit and smiling*) I couldn't believe my eyes. I'd
just come out of the sea and there she was, waving at me.
Howard I thought you weren't going to come down until the afternoon.
Bernard I wasn't. But then when I got up this morning I thought, "There isn't
any reason why I shouldn't come down earlier." The last thing I thought
was to bump into her.
Howard (*making to go off* DR) Let's go down the beach.
Bernard (*following Howard*) It's too crowded.
Howard Somewhere else, then — come on.

   Bernard and Howard exit

*Black-out. The sound of seagulls is replaced by street sounds. TheLights
come up*

Vi and Adele enter UC. *They are still shopping*

Vi I suggested that. I said to him this morning perhaps it would be a good idea
if the three of us got together. Although what I'd say to this Bernard chap,
I don't know, I'm sure.
Adele You'll think of something. Bernard? Is that his name?
Vi Yes. I've never spoken to one of them people before.
Adele (*smiling*) They've got two arms and legs the same as everyone else.
Vi Yes, I know but ——
Adele I've got two living next door to me in Putney.
Vi Have you? Oh, I don't know whether I'd like to have them live next door.
Adele They're great neighbours. I leave me key with them so they can keep
an eye on the place while I'm down here.
Vi Are they trustworthy, then?
Adele You get good and bad the same as everyone else. (*She spots something
in a window* DR) Now, I like that.
Vi That red thing?
Adele Don't you?
Vi I'm not sure.
Adele Let's go in and try it on.

They exit DR

Black-out. The street sounds give way to the sound of waves

*The Lights come up. Howard and Bernard are throwing flat pebbles across
the water. Bernard has a camera with him*

Howard (*throwing a pebble and watching it*) Seven.
Bernard (*doing the same*) Nine.
Howard You can't get nine. It's like folding paper. You can only do it seven
times. If you could do it nine times, you could reach the moon.
Bernard Where did you learn that, college?
Howard No, Bryant and May. The back of a matchbox.

Bernard takes a photograph of Howard

Bernard She took it well then.
Howard Oh, I wouldn't say that. But she took it.
Bernard Good for you.
Howard I don't know how far I've got with her but at last I've made a
breakthrough.

Bernard You won't tell her today, will you? Not while I'm here. I don't think I could face it somehow.

Howard No, tomorrow. I'm sure tomorrow's best.

Howard picks up another pebble and throws it. They both watch it. Bernard pushes Howard over in fun

Bernard One.

Bernard rushes off and Howard chases after him

Black-out. The sound of waves is replaced by disco music

The Lights come up. Coloured lights flash in time to the music

Vi is just off stage, as if in a clothes shop changing cubicle. Adele is on stage, just by the exit

Adele (*after some time*) Are you all right, Vi?

Vi (*off*) I won't be a minute.

Adele What's keeping you?

Vi (*off*) It's this bloody arm. It'll never go where I want it.

Adele Shall I come and give you some help?

Vi (*off*) No, it's all right. I think I've done it now.

A few seconds later Vi enters wearing the red dress from the shop window

Well? What do you think?

Adele Turn around.

Vi (*turning*) Look at the back — I look like a bimbo.

Adele I'm not fussed, are you?

Vi (*turning to go back into the changing cubicle*) I never liked it in the first place. What time is it?

Adele I don't know, I haven't got a watch.

Vi Must be getting on for half-past five. We'd better make our way back to the van. You will come round now, won't you? I hope Howard's looking after him — I don't think he likes him very much.

They both leave DL

Black-out. The disco music is replaced by bird-song. The Lights come up

Outside the caravan

Howard walks on from DR, *quickly followed by Bernard, who is carrying a paper bag. Howard turns and Bernard hands him the bag*

Howard What's this?
Bernard It's for you.
Howard What is it?
Bernard Open it.

Howard opens the bag, looks into it and laughs. He takes out a pair of joke glasses that have large eyes attached to springs on the front. He puts them on

Howard Great! I can keep an eye out for my mother now. (*He starts fooling around with the glasses*)
Bernard Hang on!

Bernard takes out his camera and Howard strikes a comic pose. They both laugh — but then they both gently stop. Howard takes off the glasses. They share a moment

Howard When I go, you know what it means, don't you?
Bernard To me?

Howard nods. There is a pause

I could give up my job.
Howard No, I don't want you to do that.
Bernard It wouldn't be difficult. I'm not even a good insurance agent.
Howard No, you mustn't. I don't want that.
Bernard Does it have to be all what you want?
Howard Don't you want me to go now?
Bernard Yes, of course I do — but my reasons weren't totally unselfish. (*A slight pause*) You don't want me to come with you then?
Howard (*moving away* DC) All I would like for the moment is to go back to college. That's more than enough to handle at one time. (*A slight pause*) You do understand?
Bernard (*moving to stand just behind Howard; he could almost kiss Howard's neck*) Don't I always?

There is a slight pause

Howard (*moving away* UC) I'll get the tea things.

Howard exits UC

Bernard is left standing C

Howard enters carrying a patio table. He puts this R *and heads back towards the exit*

Howard Come on — give us a hand.

Howard exits

Bernard doesn't move straight away. He then heads for the exit

Howard enters carrying two plastic chairs

Bernard exits and returns moments later with two more chairs

Howard exits

Bernard positions the chairs around the table. As he is doing this ——

Adele rushes on from L *carrying a handbag and a carrier bag from a high street shop with a dress in it. In her haste, she falls almost at Bernard's feet*

Bernard (*helping her to her feet*) Are you all right?
Adele I'm a silly cow. I'd fall over a five pence piece, me.
Bernard Come and sit down.
Adele No, I'm in a bit of a rush.
Bernard I can see that.
Adele I'm meeting some friends and I haven't got time. But thanks anyway, er ... (*she holds out her hand*) Adele.
Bernard Bernard.

Bernard and Adele shake hands

Adele Can't stop. Perhaps I'll see you again. (*She heads for the exit in a rush, then slows up as the name Bernard registers*)

Adele exits

After a moment, Howard comes out of the caravan with a plate of salmon sandwiches

Howard No one is allowed inside the van because "Madam" is changing. Salmon it is, all right?
Bernard (*sitting down at the table*) Great. I'm not that hungry though.

Howard What time are you going back?
Bernard I thought I'd go straight after tea.
Howard (*looking at Bernard*) Is there anything wrong?

Bernard stares for a moment and does not answer

I thought you wouldn't be going back until later on.
Bernard (*sotto voce*) Do you want me to stay?
Howard (*sotto*) Of course I do.
Bernard (*sotto*) I shouldn't have come. It was a mistake.
Howard (*sotto*) What's the matter?
Vi (*off*) What are you whispering, Howard?
Howard (*shouting*) Ooooh, bugger off!
Vi (*off*) What? (*A slight pause*) Who are you shouting at?
Howard A fly. There's a bloody fly on the sandwiches.
Vi (*off*) Throw it away then. Can't eat it now. Best salmon, too. Cover them
  up, Howard. Put a tea-towel over them or something till we're ready.
Howard (*whispering*) Are you — hurt?
Bernard (*after a slight pause*) That's the price.
Howard Come with me, then. It'll be all right ... Come with me.

Bernard gently shakes his head

Vi (*off*) Here you are, Howard. Have this tea-towel.
Howard (*shouting back*) It's all right, I've got one.
Bernard Why do you want me to come?
Howard (*after a slight pause*) If it wasn't for you, I wouldn't be going.
Bernard Is that your answer?

Howard doesn't reply

I could only go if I was needed. And you don't need me any more, do you?
Howard (*after a slight pause*) Look, we can't talk here. Stay longer than tea
  and maybe we'll get a chance later on. Will you?

There is a pause. Bernard smiles and nods

Vi (*off, slowly*) It's gone awful bloody quiet out there.
Howard (*moving* UC, *calling*) Hurry up with that dress or these sandwiches
  will be starting to curl.
Bernard (*going over to Howard*) When do you think you'll go?
Howard It depends on their Association and how soon they can get her a flat.
  Could be October.
Bernard It's not long to wait for us — a year.

Bernard and Howard look at each other and almost kiss

   Adele enters R

Bernard and Howard spring apart

Adele Hope I haven't missed anything.
Howard You're just in time. Adele, this is Mr Fowler, our friend from back
   home.
Adele Yes, we've met.
Howard (*amazed*) Have you?
Adele I had a bit of an accident just now and he helped me to my feet. I'm
   sorry, you did tell me your name but I've forgot.
Bernard } (*together*) { Dennis.
Howard }   { Peter.
Bernard } (*together*) { Peter.
Howard }   { Dennis.
Adele Pleased to meet you, "Bernard". (*She laughs*)

*Eventually Bernard and Howard see the funny side and join in with the
laughter*

   This is *the* Bernard, I take it.

Howard and Bernard are reluctant to confirm this

   It's all right, mum's the word, she won't get nothing out of me.
Howard We are going to tell her, aren't we?
Bernard That's right.
Howard Only later.
Adele Makes no difference to me, love. (*She moves* UC) In the van then, is
   she?
Howard Trying on her new dress.
Vi (*off*) I'm coming out. Are you ready?
Adele Come on, Vi, let's have a butcher's.

They wait

   *Vi enters from the caravan wearing a navy blue dress with white spots. She
positions herself in front of the others and waits for their comments*

Vi Well, what do you think?

Adele I think it's smashing.

Vi Mr Fowler?

Bernard Very nice.

Vi What do you say, Howard?

Howard (*after a pause*) You look like a domino.

Vi Right, it's back tomorrow.

Adele Don't say that, Howard. It's very nice, Vi, honest.

Howard (*rushing to Vi*) Yeah, it's very nice. (*He puts his arm around her and gives her a kiss*)

Vi Well, as long as you like it. Right, who's going to be mother?

Adele Listen, I've had an idea. We won't bother with tea. Not now since you're all dolled up and everything. What do you say we go down the pub for an hour?

Howard Yeah, why not?

Vi No. I don't go to them places.

Adele You don't have to go in, Vi. We'll just sit out in the beer garden.

Vi No, I don't think so.

Adele Come on, don't be an old stick-in-the-mud.

Vi But I'm hungry.

Adele You can have something to eat down there. What do you say? You can have a cocktail.

Vi No, I don't eat chicken.

They all laugh

What have I said now?

Adele Grab her, Howard — we'll drag her down there.

Vi What about the salmon sandwiches?

Adele (*picking up the sandwiches and heading for the caravan*) I'll stick them in the van. We'll eat those when we get back.

Bernard and Howard pick up Vi under the arms and carry her towards the exit L

Vi Watch my arm, Howard — my arm. And my bag. Where's my bag?

Adele I'll bring your bloody bag.

Adele exits UC. Vi, Howard and Bernard go off L

The Lights fade

The sound of bird-song is replaced by pub or juke-box music

The patio table and chairs are moved from their position R to C. A row of coloured lights is hung between the two flats

SCENE 4

The pub

The stage Lights and the row of coloured lights come up. The music decreases in volume, becoming a background sound suggesting a pub interior

Adele, Howard, Bernard and Vi are sitting at the table. Both Adele and Vi have bags with them. Everyone seems pretty jolly. Adele is in the middle of telling a joke

Adele No, listen — listen. So he asked the farmer if he could give him some petrol and while the farmer was filling up the can, the man said: "On my way up here through your fields, something kept running in front of me. I couldn't see what it was because it was going so fast," and the farmer said, "Yes, well I'll tell you what that is: we're a large family, you see — there's me and the wife, and the six children — and for our Sunday dinner we have chicken and we all like a leg each, so what I've done, I've crossed a chicken with a spider." And the man said "Really? What does it taste like?" And the farmer said, "I don't know — I haven't caught the bugger yet."

They all laugh

Howard (*standing*) Come on, drink up.

They do

(*To Bernard*) Same again, Mr Fowler?

Bernard nods

(*To Vi*) What about you, Mam? Another pineapple juice?
Vi No, I think I'll have something different this time.
Adele That's right, Vi, you enjoy yourself.
Vi I'll have — a tomato juice.

They all laugh

Howard Adele?
Adele I'm not sure what I want. I think I'll come to the bar with you, Howard.

Howard and Adele exit to the bar L leaving Bernard and Vi at the table

Vi (*watching them both walk off*) She's a hell of a girl, i'n' she?

Bernard A live wire, yes.

Vi It's a pity she lives so far away — her and Howard get on like a house on fire. It's someone like her he needs, see. Get him back on the right track. (*She turns to Bernard*) Between you and me, Mr Fowler, I feel I can talk to ... It seems a bit silly me still calling you Mr Fowler when we've known each other so long. From now on you call me Vi, right? And I'll call you ...

Bernard (*after a slight pause*) Er — Robert.

Vi Right, Robert. Come and sit by here, Robert.

Bernard hesitates

Come on, come and sit by me.

He does

Now where was I? Howard, yes. Between you and me, Robert, I'm a bit worried about Howard.

Bernard shows every sign of feeling very uncomfortable

The thing is, he's on about going back to college. Well, that's bad enough but I think I might be able to cope with that. It's this other problem he's got that I don't know how to handle. (*A slight pause*) You see our Howard is convinced he's a bit ... (*she rolls her eyes and cocks her head to one side*) you know. (*She repeats the action*) Do you know?

Bernard (*swallowing hard*) Yes, I think so.

Vi Call me Vi.

Bernard Vi.

Vi And I'm worried that he doesn't really want to go back to college at all. I think he just wants to go away and live with this Bernard.

Bernard (*slightly panicked*) Bernard?

Vi That's his name. In fact, I'm convinced it's him that's put all this business back into our Howard's head.

Bernard Really?

Vi Well, my problem is, I've told Howard that I think we should talk about it, the three of us like — but I don't know if I can, see, because I think if I was to see this Bernard now I'd wring his bloody neck. (*A slight pause*) What do you think then, Robert? Should I see him or not?

Bernard (*after a pause, not knowing where to begin*) I'm — I'm sure he's not entirely to blame. (*Before Vi can ask him another question, he carries on*) Howard might be young, but he does know his own mind. At least, that's the way he seems to me. (*A slight pause*) This Bernard chap, he might have encouraged Howard to go back to college — but I wouldn't have thought he'd be going with him.

Vi Don't you? Why?

Bernard (*after a slight pause*) It's just — er — a feeling I've got. Just a feeling, that's all.

Vi So you think I should meet him, then?

Bernard (*panicking again*) Well, I don't know about that. Anyway, perhaps Bernard — this Bernard — doesn't want to meet you. (*He tries to make light of the following*) Especially if he thinks you might want to strangle him.

Vi Well he won't know that, will he? Not till he sees me.

They laugh, Vi quite heartily; the laugh fades and they both sigh. There is a slight pause

No, I reckon he's a bad influence on Howard. He was a nice boy before he got involved with him.

Bernard I'm sure he doesn't — doesn't mean any harm. If he's involved with — er — where are the others?

Vi They won't be long. You were saying?

Bernard (*after a slight pause*) Perhaps he's not as you see him at all.

Vi Who?

Bernard This — er ...

Vi Bernard?

Bernard Yes. Maybe he's interested in Howard in more than just the way you think.

Vi What way?

Bernard He might feel about Howard in much the same way as you do.

Vi Me?

Bernard Wanting him to get on and that. Wanting what's best for him.

Vi Oh, right ... I reckon I should talk then?

Before Bernard can answer, Howard and Adele return from the bar with the drinks

They sit at the table and sort the drinks out. Bernard can't wait to leave. Howard puts Bernard's drink in front of him

Bernard Did I ask for the same thing? I fancy something different now. Don't worry — I'll get it.

Bernard rushes off

Howard (*sensing something is wrong; to Vi*) Everything all right?

Vi Yes, yes. (*Of Bernard's drink*) He's not going to waste that now, is he? (*To Adele*) He's only an insurance man, but he's doing very well for himself. Did I tell you he owns our caravan?

Adele I think you might have mentioned it, Vi, yeah.

Vi He's not married. Lives with his sister and her husband. Nice boy.

Adele My heart turned over at that bar. There's this fella serving there — he's a dead ringer for me late husband. Same shape 'tache and all. I couldn't get over it.

Howard looks in the direction of the bar. During the following it is obvious that he has seen Bernard and that Bernard is trying to communicate something to him which he is trying to understand. Howard mouths things back to Bernard — as yet unseen by Vi

Vi Must have been an awful time for you. It was for me I know.

Adele Been four years now.

Vi How old was he?

Adele Only twenty-three.

Vi Young.

Adele No one could understand it. He was one of these keep-fit fanatics.

Vi How did it happen?

Adele He was out in the street.

Vi And a car knocked him down?

Adele No, he was jogging and he dropped dead.

Vi (*becoming aware of Howard*) What's the matter, Howard?

Howard (*caught*) What? Nothing.

Vi Who are you talking to?

Howard Mr Fowler. I'm trying to catch his attention. I want some crisps.

Vi Yes. I fancy some crisps as well. Go and get four packets.

Vi hands Howard her purse

Howard exits to the bar

After a slight pause

Well, it's almost over now — the holiday. It's Thursday already.

Adele Had a good time, have you?

Vi Yes, I've enjoyed myself. I didn't think I would, mind, but all in all it hasn't been too bad. I'll have to start packing tomorrow.

Adele I'll give you my address. (*She reaches for her bag on the table and gets out a little notepad and pencil during the following*) You'll keep in touch now, won't you? Let me know how you are and how Howard's getting on.

Vi Course I will. (*Confidentially*) I've had a little chat to our friend while you and Howard were at the bar. (*She gestures to Bernard's empty seat*)

Adele Oh yeah.

Vi I think I've sorted it out.

Adele You have?

Vi I'm going to talk to him.

Adele Good for you.

Vi Never let it be said that Violet Davies isn't a reasonable woman.

Adele So it's all out in the open then? I'm ever so glad. I knew it would be all right once they'd told you.

Howard and Bernard return from the bar with Bernard's new drink and four packets of crisps

Vi Told me what?

Adele Bernard!

The boys stop dead in their tracks, do an immediate about turn and run back off in the direction of the bar

Vi watches them go

Black-out. The volume of the pub music rises

SCENE 5

Outside the caravan

The music fades. The Lights come up

After a moment, Howard enters from the caravan with two suitcases which he puts down on the ground. He heads back towards the caravan

Vi enters from the caravan carrying a tubular folding chair

Vi passes Howard; their eyes meet and there is a brief frosty moment between them

Howard exits into the caravan and returns with a holdall, which he places down beside the other cases. As he does so:

Vi throws her folded chair down on the ground. The noise makes Howard turn his head to look at her. Vi puts her foot on part of the chair and by bending and holding the other part of the chair opens it in a manner which shows us she has developed her own method of doing it. She opens the chair fully, sits in it and is silent

There is a slight pause

Howard I gather you're all ready to go then?

Vi doesn't answer; she turns her head in the opposite direction

Look, don't you think you're being a bit silly taking this attitude?

Again, she doesn't reply

I'm going over to say cheerio to Adele — are you coming? (*He waits for an answer*)

Nothing is forthcoming. Howard turns to leave

Vi I said "So long" this morning.
Howard Please don't be like this. (*A slight pause*) Try and understand ——
Vi Have you locked that caravan? Because I don't want him coming back to me saying it's been burgled.
Howard You know I would have told you eventually. It was a bit unfortunate you found out like you did.
Vi Unfortunate? I'll say it was un-bloody-fortunate! I've never been so embarrassed in all my life. I'd only taken him into my confidence five minutes before.
Howard If you felt soft imagine how he felt. After you made that ridiculous scene, I wasn't feeling that good either.
Vi If anything is ridiculous, it's the way this whole thing has turned out. (*A slight pause*) I should have known — it should have clicked with me. It had to be someone who came to the house, you don't see no bugger else.
Howard Does it really matter who it is?
Vi Of course it does — to me. And to make matters worse, I've just spent a week in his caravan. If I had my way, I'd ask him for that hundred pounds back.
Howard He didn't charge us.

Vi looks at Howard

He let me have it free. See? I told you I could cheat, didn't I?
Vi (*almost mumbling*) And to think I bought him a new milk jug and sugar bowl and all.

Howard And what about Adele? God knows she felt embarrassed, being
the one to let it slip.

Vi I've sorted it all out with Adele. I don't blame her at all. And she wasn't
that embarrassed anyway, 'cos she told me she laughed like a drain when
she got back to her van.

Howard (*moving behind Vi and standing to her* L) Well, you've got to admit
it, there is a funny side to it. You might not be able to laugh at it now, but
in a couple of years ——

Vi Howard, if I'm still alive and kicking at seventy, I won't be able to laugh
at that lot.

Howard (*after a slight pause*) He's not a bad chap. I am what I am through
no fault of Bernard's. It's not fair to blame him.

Vi Well, I hope you don't think it's my fault.

Howard (*kneeling beside Vi*) Of course it's not. I don't understand it myself.
I think it's got something to do with the genes.

Vi (*after a slight pause*) Howard, how can you be like you are because of
a pair of bloody jeans.

Howard looks at Vi and smiles. He puts his hands on hers

Howard Oh Mam — you're priceless. (*A slight pause. He gets up and makes
to exit* R) I'm just going to say ta-ra to Adele.

Vi Don't be long or we'll miss the bus.

Howard (*stopping dead in his tracks*) Ah!

Vi What?

Howard Well, after all that confusion on Thursday, I forgot to tell Bernard
not to come down.

Vi You shouldn't have to have told him. After the way I spoke to him there's
no way he's going to come all the way down here to fetch me.

Howard He will.

Vi Well, I don't want him to. Phone him and tell him not to bother.

Howard I can't do that. Anyway he's on his way — in fact, he'll be here
before long.

Vi He'll make a journey for nothing then because I'm not going back in his
car.

Howard That's ridiculous.

Vi I don't care what it is.

Howard (*a little impatiently*) You'll be quicker in the car.

Vi I don't care how long it takes — I'll walk before I'll go back with him.

Howard (*moving behind her again, losing his temper*) You arranged it.
You're the one who conned him into offering in the first place.

Vi That's before I knew who he was.

Howard He's still the same person. He hasn't changed.

Vi He has in my eyes.
Howard (*kneeling beside her again*) Please come back with us.
Vi Oh ... it's us now, is it? Going back with him, are you?
Howard Yes.
Vi (*determinedly*) Fair enough. (*She stands*)
Howard Where are you going?
Vi To the bus station.
Howard Don't be silly — you can't go back on your own.
Vi (*walking* US) Watch me.
Howard (*shouting*) You can't.

Adele rushes on R

Adele All packed and ready to go, are we?
Howard (*to Adele*) See if you can talk some sense into her.
Vi (*stopping briefly*) I came on the bus — and I'll go home on the bus. Ta-ra, Adele.

Vi turns and leaves

Howard Don't do this. (*He moves to follow after Vi*)

Adele grabs Howard's arm and prevents him from leaving

Adele No, you mustn't.

Howard looks at Adele

You mustn't.

Black-out

SCENE 6

On the coach

The Lights come back up. The sounds of a coach interior can be heard

Vi is seated, talking to an imaginary person who is sitting on her R. *Vi has a bag of sweets with her*

Vi I always think a week is enough, don't you? A fortnight is all right if you've got the money, that's what I say. You are ... Have one of these. (*She*

offers a bag of sweets) Coconut mushrooms. ... Don't you? Oh, I love 'em,
I do. What about the little boy? Does he want one? ... Shy, I expect. I got
one in the house — he used to be the same when he was his age. How old
is he — nine? ... Ten? Twenty-one mine is. Been home with me for a year.
Helped me get back on my feet after my stroke. ... Yes, all down my left
side. It's coming back slowly but it all takes time. Howard, that's my boy,
he's going back to college soon. Wants to be a teacher. I'd rather have him
home with me of course, but it's not fair, is it? Mustn't stand in their way,
must we? And I'm glad he's going back really. I wouldn't like people to
think I'd stopped him. Couldn't live with that. (*Meaning the boy*) Tired is
he? Almost dropping off. Yes. I can't myself, but you carry on.

*There is a pause. She looks around for someone else to talk to and spots
someone sitting in front*

Excuse me. (*She reacts as if she has gained the person's attention*) Fancy
a coconut mushroom?

Black-out. The coach interior sounds are replaced by the noise of traffic

SCENE 7

Outside Vi's and Howard's house

*The Lights come up. Howard is sitting outside the house. He has all the
luggage around him*

Vi enters DL, *with her handbag. She sees Howard and stops*

Vi What are you doing out here?
Howard I haven't got a key. You've got it.

There is a slight pause. Vi laughs to herself and walks towards Howard

You're all right, then?
Vi Well, I'm here, aren't I?
Howard How did you manage on the bus?
Vi Very well. The driver said it was the quietest crowd he'd had for a long
time. I think I talked every bugger to sleep.

They both laugh

Now, where's the key? (*She tries to get the key out of her bag*)

Howard moves to get the key out for her

Vi No, it's all right.

They look at each other

 (*Putting her hand to Howard's face*) It's all right.

They share something. We know it's going to be all right with them

Black-out. The traffic noise fades and the music that began the play comes up

SCENE 8

The living-room of Vi's new home

The music fades; the Lights come up

There are two armchairs on stage, each with a small table by it. On one of the tables is a small intercom unit. Bernard is sitting in one of the armchairs entering up his book. Vi is off stage; her voice comes from the direction of the kitchen

Vi (*off*) So it's no sugar, then?
Bernard That's right.
Vi (*off*) I've made Welsh cakes.
Bernard Have you? Smashing.
Vi (*off*) But if you're cutting down ——
Bernard One is all right.
Vi (*off*) Some diet.

  Vi enters pushing a tea trolley with tea things and a plate of Welsh cakes on it

Bernard Will you be wanting to take out another endowment now that this one's matured?
Vi Might as well. What do you think? (*Before he can answer, she speaks again*) I'm not paying any more, mind. Two pound a week is enough.
Bernard You should up it a bit.
Vi Two pound fifty then and that's my lot.

Bernard hands Vi a cheque

Bernard One thousand, six hundred and seventy-three pounds. Make sure you don't lose it.

Vi I won't have it long enough to lose it. It's going straight up the bank now.

Bernard That's right. Thought about what you're going to do with it?

Vi (*taking a cup of tea and a Welsh cake from the trolley and heading for her usual chair*) Well, I'm going away for a week with the Stroke Club, but that's not until August. Hey, guess where we're going? Tenby.

Bernard smiles

(*Sitting*) Help yourself.

Bernard helps himself to tea and a Welsh cake. There is a slight pause

Have you heard from Howard?

Bernard Have you?

Vi I had a letter yesterday.

Bernard And me.

Vi I hope he writes to you more often than he does to me. That's the first letter I've had this month.

Bernard He writes to you regular, he told me.

Vi Ay, once a month regular. He's working hard, he says.

Bernard It'll be exams soon.

Vi June, innit?

Bernard nods

I don't know what he'll do after that, mind.

They look at each other. Bernard has no idea of the answer to that question either and she can see this in his face

There is a buzz from the intercom. Vi presses the button

Vi Hallo?

The voice of the warden — female — can either be played live over the intercom or can be pre-recorded

Warden's Voice Hallo, Vi? I'm going down the shops. I'm just checking to see if you want anything.

Vi No, not for me. I'm going to the bank myself this afternoon.

Warden's Voice Right you are.

The intercom clicks off

Vi That was Vera. She always rings and asks if there's anything I want. She pops in in the evening too. She often spends an hour in here with me. (*Confidentially*) She's having a bit of bother with her son. Same sort of trouble as you and our Howard. I've told her: I said, "Now, there's nothing you can do — if it's in him it's in him. I know it's not easy to come to terms with", I said, "but you will eventually. I mean, look at me."

Bernard So you told her about Howard?

Vi Well, yes. Oh, it made her feel ever so much better knowing somebody else had the same kind of problem, you know. And it did me the world of good too. (*A thought strikes her*) Oh, I didn't mention you, mind. (*Reassuringly*) I just said Howard was involved with a friend.

Bernard (*after a slight pause*) I'm selling my caravan, Vi.

Vi Are you?

Bernard I'm getting a new one.

Vi A bigger one this time, I hope.

Bernard (*laughing*) The thing is, I'm not sure where to put it. I don't know if I want to keep it in Tenby.

Vi (*quickly*) Bournemouth's nice.

Bernard I quite fancy Torquay.

Vi It's lovely and clean in Bournemouth. June Watkins, she's the friend I go to the pictures with on a Tuesday, she went to Bournemouth last year. She said it's lovely. Plenty of shows and everything.

Bernard Well, they've got shows in Torquay.

Vi It's up to you of course. (*Almost to herself*) But I've never been to Bournemouth.

Bernard laughs. Vi looks at him

Bernard Oh, Vi — you're priceless.

Simultaneously they dunk their Welsh cakes and eat them

Black-out

FURNITURE AND PROPERTY LIST

ACT I
SCENE 1

On stage: Carpet
Two fireside chairs. *On chair* L: walking stick
Two small tables. *On table* L: open packet of sweets, telephone. *On table* R: cup and saucer
Fire irons
Book for **Howard**
Apple for **Howard**

SCENE 2

Strike: Sweets, cup and saucer, book, apple core

Set: Radio (with practical speaker)
On L *table*: Insurance account book
Ewbank cleaner for **Vi**

Off stage: Attaché case (**Bernard**)
Bottle of milk (**Howard**)

SCENE 3

Strike: Radio, account book, Ewbank cleaner

Set: Dining chair. *On it*: **Howard**'s shirt
Howard's shoes
TV remote contol unit for **Vi**

Off stage: Towel (**Howard**)
Battery shaver (**Howard**)
Flask (**Howard**)

Personal: **Howard**: comb

Scene 4

Strike: All living-room props, including carpet

Scene 5

Set: Two coach seats
     Holdall for **Vi**. *In it*: foil package of sandwiches

Scene 6

Strike: All props from Scene 5

Off stage: Shoulder bag containing key (**Vi**)
     Several bags, holdalls, folding chairs and other luggage (**Howard**)

Personal: **Vi**: sweet, walking stick (used throughout)

Scene 7

Off stage: Folded sun lounger, sun tan lotion, book et cetera (**Howard**)

Scene 8

Set: Telephone box
     Municipal waste-paper bin

Off stage: Two ice cream cornets

Personal: Personal stereo (**Girl**)

Scene 9

Strike: Telephone box
     Waste paper bin

Set: Caravan interior
     Fish and chips for **Howard** and **Vi**

ACT II
SCENE 1

Strike:	Caravan interior
Set:	Tap Makeshift washing line with pegs Skimpy underwear for **Adele**
Off stage:	**Howard**'s swimming things

SCENE 2

Strike:	All props from SCENE 1
Off stage:	Deckchair, air-bed, bag containing towels, a flask of tea and cups (**Howard**) Clothes and towel (**Bernard**)
Personal:	**Vi**: handbag **Bernard**: goggles and snorkel

SCENE 3

Strike:	All props from SCENE 2
Off stage:	Camera (**Bernard**) Paper bag containing joke glasses (**Bernard**) Patio table (**Howard**) Two plastic chairs (**Howard**) Two plastic chairs (**Bernard**) Handbag, carrier bag containing dress (**Adele**) Plate of salmon sandwiches (**Howard**)

SCENE 4

Re-set;	Patio table and chairs
Set:	Row of practical coloured lights Drinks
Off stage:	More drinks Four packets of crisps
Personal:	Handbag containing purse (**Vi**) Handbag containing notepad, pencil (**Adele**)

SCENE 5

Strike: All props from SCENE 4

Off stage:	Two suitcases (**Howard**)
	Tubular folding chair (**Vi**)
	Holdall (**Howard**)

SCENE 6

Strike: All props from SCENE 5

Set: Coach seats

Personal: **Vi**: handbag, bag of sweets

SCENE 7

Strike: All props from SCENE 6

Set: Luggage

Personal: **Vi**: handbag

SCENE 8

Strike: All props from SCENE 7

Set: Two armchairs
Two small tables. *On one*: small practical intercom unit
Account book and cheque for **Bernard**

Off stage: Tea trolley with tea things and plate of Welsh cakes on it (**Vi**)

LIGHTING PLOT

Practical fittings required: row of coloured lights
Various interior and exterior settings

ACT I, Scene 1

To open: Darkness

Cue 1	Music *House lights down*	(Page 1)
Cue 2	When ready *Stage lights up; general interior lighting*	(Page 1)
Cue 3	**Vi**: " ... something's beginning with **Howard.**" *Black-out*	(Page 5)

ACT I, Scene 2

To open: Darkness

Cue 4	Local radio station plays *Lights up; general interior lighting*	(Page 5)
Cue 5	**Howard** looks up and out *Black-out*	(Page 10)

ACT I, Scene 3

To open: Darkness

Cue 6	When ready *Lights up; general interior lighting*	(Page 10)
Cue 7	**Howard**: "One egg or two?" *Lights fade to black-out*	(Page 18)

ACT I, SCENE 4

To open: Darkness

No cues

ACT I, SCENE 5

To open: Darkness

| Cue 8 | Jolly banjo music | (Page 20) |
| | *Lights up; coach interior* | |

| Cue 9 | **Howard**: "Oh my God!" | (Page 22) |
| | *Black-out* | |

ACT I, SCENE 6

To open: Darkness

| Cue 10 | When ready | (Page 22) |
| | *Lights up; general exterior lighting* | |

| Cue 11 | **Adele** exits | (Page 26) |
| | *Lights dim* | |

ACT I, SCENE 7

To open: Dim light

| Cue 12 | Sound of bird-song gets louder | (Page 26) |
| | *Lights brighten to suggest sunshine* | |

| Cue 13 | **Adele** exits | (Page 30) |
| | *Black-out* | |

ACT I, SCENE 8

To open: Darkness

| Cue 14 | When ready | (Page 30) |
| | *Lights up; general exterior lighting* | |

| Cue 15 | **Howard** tosses his ice-cream into the bin | (Page 35) |
| | *Lights fade to black-out* | |

ACT I, Scene 9

To open: Darkness

Cue 16	Music fades	(Page 35)
	Lights come up dimly; caravan interior lighting	
Cue 17	Violin music	(Page 39)
	Black-out	

ACT II, Scene 1

To open: Darkness

Cue 18	Violin music plays	(Page 40)
	Lights up; general exterior lighting	
Cue 19	**Adele** exits; **Vi** is left pondering	(Page 43)
	Lights fade to black-out	

Act II, Scene 2

To open: Darkness

Cue 20	Beach sounds	(Page 43)
	Lights up; general exterior lighting	
Cue 21	Beach sounds get louder	(Page 46)
	Lights fade to black-out and almost immediately come up again	
Cue 22	**Howard** lets the towel go	(Page 51)
	Black-out	

ACT II, Scene 3

To open: Darkness

Cue 23	Street sounds	(Page 51)
	Lights up; general exterior lighting	
Cue 24	**Vi** and **Adele** exit	(Page 52)
	Black-out	
Cue 25	Street sounds give way to seagulls	(Page 52)
	Lights up; general exterior lighting	

Cue 26	**Bernard** and **Howard** exit *Black-out*	(Page 53)
Cue 27	Seagulls replaced by street sounds *Lights up; general exterior lighting*	(Page 53)
Cue 28	**Vi** and **Adele** exit *Black-out*	(Page 53)
Cue 29	Street sounds give way to waves *Lights up; general exterior lighting*	(Page 53)
Cue 30	**Bernard** and **Howard** exit *Black-out*	(Page 54)
Cue 31	Sound of waves replaced by disco music *Lights up; general interior lighting with coloured flashing lights*	(Page 54)
Cue 32	**Adele** and **Vi** exit *Black-out*	(Page 54)
Cue 33	Disco music replaced by bird-song *Lights up; general exterior lighting*	(Page 54)
Cue 34	**Vi**, **Howard** and **Bernard** exit L *Lights fade*	(Page 59)

ACT II, Scene 4

To open: Dim light

Cue 35	When ready *Stage lights, and practical coloured lights, up*	(Page 60)
Cue 36	**Vi** watches **Howard** and **Bernard** go *Black-out*	(Page 64)

ACT II, Scene 5

To open: Darkness

Cue 37	Music fades *Lights up; general exterior lighting*	(Page 64)
Cue 38	**Adele**: "You mustn't." *Black-out*	(Page 67)

ACT II, Scene 6

To open: Darkness

Cue 39	When ready	(Page 67)
	Lights up; coach interior lighting	

Cue 40	**Vi**: "Fancy a coconut mushroom?"	(Page 68)
	Black-out	

ACT II, Scene 7

To open: Darkness

Cue 41	Traffic noise	(Page 68)
	Lights up; general exterior lighting	

Cue 42	**Vi** and **Howard** share a moment	(Page 69)
	Black-out	

ACT II, Scene 8

To open: Darkness

Cue 43	Music fades	(Page 69)
	Lights up; general interior lighting	

Cue 44	**Vi** and **Bernard** eat their Welsh cakes	(Page 71)
	Black-out	

EFFECTS PLOT

ACT I

Cue 1	When ready *Music*	(Page 1)
Cue 2	Black-out *Violin music, overlapping with, then superceded by,* *local radio station*	(Page 5)
Cue 3	Lights come up *Fade radio sound to a very quiet background* *noise from onstage radio*	(Page 5)
Cue 4	**Howard** switches off the radio *Cut radio sound*	(Page 8)
Cue 5	Black-out *Violin music*	(Page 10)
Cue 6	Lights up *Change music to "Emmerdale" theme*	(Page 10)
Cue 7	**Howard**: "It's bloody Bernard, right?" Terrible pause *Telephone rings*	(Page 18)
Cue 8	**Howard** answers the phone *Cut telephone sound*	(Page 18)
Cue 9	Lights fade to black-out *Sound of clock ticking; starts quietly and gains in volume*	(Page 18)
Cue 10	Scene 4 *Dialogue, clock ticking, alarm ringing and* *jolly banjo music as pp. 18-20*	(Page 18)

Cue 11	Lights come up on **Vi** and **Howard** *Fade music, bring up sounds of coach interior*	(Page 20)
Cue 12	Lights come up *Fade coach sounds; bring up bird-song*	(Page 22)
Cue 13	Lights dim *Increase volume of bird-song*	(Page 26)
Cue 14	Lights brighten to suggest sunshine *Return volume of bird-song to previous level*	(Page 26)
Cue 15	Black-out *Very loud heavy metal music*	(Page 30)
Cue 16	Lights up *Fade music*	(Page 30)
Cue 17	**Vi**: " ... bugger all left." *Music; possibly "Beanfields" by the Penguin Café Orchestra*	(Page 34)
Cue 18	When ready *Fade music*	(Page 35)
Cue 19	**Vi**: "Howard?" *Violin music — very quiet*	(Page 39)

ACT II

Cue 20	When ready *Violin music*	(Page 40)
Cue 21	Lights come up *Music fades*	(Page 40)
Cue 22	Black-out *"California Girls" by the Beach Boys*	(Page 43)
Cue 23	When ready *Fade music; replace with beach sounds*	(Page 43)
Cue 24	**Howard**'s laugh becomes hearty *Beach sounds get louder, drowning **Howard** out*	(Page 46)
Cue 25	Black-out *Fade beach noises; bring up street sounds*	(Page 51)

Cue 26	Black-out *Fade street sounds; bring up call of seagulls*	(Page 52)
Cue 27	Black-out *Fade seagulls; bring up street sounds*	(Page 53)
Cue 28	Black-out *Fade street sounds; bring up waves*	(Page 53)
Cue 29	Black-out *Fade waves; bring up disco music*	(Page 54)
Cue 30	Black-out *Fade disco music; bring up bird-song*	(Page 54)
Cue 31	Lights fade *Fade bird-song; bring up pub or juke-box music*	(Page 59)
Cue 32	Lights come up on pub *Decrease volume of music to background noise*	(Page 60)
Cue 33	Black-out *Increase volume of pub music*	(Page 64)
Cue 34	When ready *Fade music*	(Page 64)
Cue 35	Lights come up on coach *Coach interior sounds*	(Page 67)
Cue 36	Black-out *Fade coach interior sounds; bring up traffic noise*	(Page 68)
Cue 37	Black-out *Fade traffic noise; bring up music that began play*	(Page 69)
Cue 38	When ready *Fade music*	(Page 69)
Cue 39	**Bernard** and **Vi** look at each other *Buzz from intercom; dialogue, live or recorded,* *as pp. 70-71*	(Page 70)